D0904829

Writing and Fantasy in Proust

La Place de la madeleine: Ecriture et fantasme chez Proust

by Serge Doubrovsky

Translated by Carol Mastrangelo Bové, with Paul A. Bové

Preface by Carol Mastrangelo Bové

with an Afterword by Paul A. Bové

Writing and Fantasy in

Proust

La Place de la madeleine

University of Nebraska Press

Lincoln & London

Originally published as *La Place de la Madeleine:
Ecriture et fantasme chez Proust*, © Editions Mercure de France 1974.

The paper in this book meets the minimum requirements of American National Standard
for Information Sciences—Permanence of Paper for
Printed Library Materials, ANSI Z39.48-1984.

Library of Congress Cataloging-in-Publication Data
Doubrovsky, Serge.
Writing and fantasy in Proust = La place de la
Madeleine (La Place de la Madeleine, écriture et
fantasme chez Proust).
Translation of: La place de la Madeleine.
Bibliography: p.
1. Proust, Marcel, 1871-1922. A la recherche du
temps perdu   2. Psychoanalysis and literature.
3. Fantasy in literature.   I. Title.
PQ 2631.R63A786413   1986   843'.912   85-31823
ISBN 0-8032-1670-X (alkaline paper)

Contents

Translator's Preface

Serge Doubrovsky's *La Place de la madeleine: Ecriture et fantasme chez Proust*, a psychoanalytic reading of the *Recherche* originally published in French in 1974, follows two other fine volumes on literature: a study of Corneille, *Corneille et la dialectique du héros*, and an evaluation of recent developments in French criticism, *Pourquoi la nouvelle critique?*[1] He is also the author of a number of experimental novels which have been given a good deal of attention recently in France, including *Le Jour S* and *La Dispersion.*[2]

Doubrovsky's *Madeleine* is significant both as a psychoanalytic approach to literature in general and as a contribution to the study of Proust. His Freudian methodology is not a representative psychoanalytic approach, however. The significant differences between Doubrovsky and such other analysts as Gaston Bachelard and Charles Mauron are that for the former (1) the text exists in time as an alternating series of conscious and unconscious desires, and (2) special linguistic properties like metaphor and metonymy shape the narrative so that the reader may follow the discontinuous alternations of the psyche.[3]

Beyond the importance of Doubrovsky's methodology lies his importance for the study of the *Recherche*. Among the *Madeleine*'s chief accomplishments is that in the context of predominantly atemporal readings of the novel, it deals with Proustian fantasy as a series of transformations emerging in time. The structure that Doubrovsky uncovers in the *Recherche* is temporal to the extent that it consists of the fluctuating movements of the psyche, which exist as a sequence of events succeeding each other in time.[4] In existential terms that make the novel immediately relevant to the reader, Doubrovsky reads the *Recherche* as the textual equivalent of the experience of living in time as a contingent being in a state of physical and psychological flux, as a series of different selves. He sees Proust's novel as the discontinuous projections of a series of selves that alternately desire the mother and murder her. Like Sartre in *Saint-Genet*, Doubrovsky demonstrates that consciousness constantly alternates between, on the one hand, the attempt to objectify or reify its existence, to create an identity, and on the other hand, the attempt to change or reject reification, to refuse any possible identity in writing. Briefly stated, Doubrovsky finds the source of fragmentation in the interplay between the conscious and the unconscious domains and in the opposing movements that operate within these domains.

Although it is obvious that the narrator of the *Recherche* exists in time and suffers acutely from the changes it brings, many critics minimize the role of temporal process when they interpret Proust. They do so in part because of the apparently teleological structure of the work. For these critics, the final epiphany to which the uneven paving stones give rise seems to fuse the disparate moments of the narrator's consciousness into an identifiable self and to offer the model of a kind of atemporal literature based upon recollection. More specifically, critics have often identified the Symbolist narrator, who does possess many of Proust's own attitudes, with the structure of the *Recherche* as a whole. Harry Levin points out that Valéry Larbaud's early reading of Proust as a Symbolist entirely ignores his social concerns. Levin's work raises a disagreement that remains to this day unresolved in Proust studies. Larbaud's judgment, together with the early commentaries of Edmund Wilson and Joseph Frank, began a practice followed more recently by Proustians who write in a variety of traditions—New Critical, phenomenological, existential, structural, or sociological: Germaine Brée, Georges Poulet, Jean-Pierre Richard, René Girard, Jeffrey Mehlman, Gilles Deleuze, and Pierre Zima, to take a few notable examples. Although some of these critics are aware of differences between the narrator and the entire novel, they view the *Recherche* in one way or another as a fixed formal structure.[5]

Such a view characterizes both the French Symbolists (see Mallarmé's *L'Après-midi d'un faune*, for instance) and Proust's narrator: they believe that the formal structure of their work reveals a glimpse of the psyche and that it will transform the flux of subjective states into the permanence of an aesthetic object. Yet unconscious desire qualifies the narrator's voice in the *Recherche*, as Doubrovsky's analysis makes clear.

In his version of existential psychoanalysis, René Girard seems to be aware of this qualification and to describe a temporal dimension in Proust in that the narrator moves through distinct stages as he transforms himself into the writer.[6] In addition, Girard indicates a dynamic quality in the *Recherche* when he analyzes individual moments in the narrator's process of discovery. This process includes shifts from one idol to another and, within these shifts, alternating episodes of depression and euphoria as the psyche (1) suffers disillusionment in its vain attempts to imitate the Other (for example, to displace Albertine's supposed lovers during her stay with him in Paris) and (2) enjoys the calm and distanced pleasure of the artist who fuses subject and object in a coherent synthesis (the madeleine episode, the writing of the passage on the Martinville spires, and the like).

Underlying the changes Girard describes in this history of the birth of a writer, however, is a disturbing portrait of a stable psyche. For Girard, it is a fundamental fact of existence that we attempt to transform ourselves into an idealized version of the Other. In an age when belief in God is rare, the unconscious satisfies the urge for transcendence by conferring divinity upon the Other and by attempting to become this Other. The most precious attribute of the divine is the permanent, self-sufficient, necessary existence it enjoys. At the end of a long apprenticeship, the novelist discovers the hidden motive in his desire, reveals it in his work, and in so doing enjoys the only kind of fulfillment available to him. This fulfillment is that of the artist who, looking back over his past life, recognizes the existence of the Other and its role in his fantasies, and succeeds in uniting this experience with his own.

Girard interprets Proust's experience as a variation of this psychological model. It becomes clear that Girard's understanding of the psyche and of the novel in which it is revealed is basically static—the novelist's desire obeys an unchanging system of laws. No important differences surface in Girard's analyses of Cervantes, Stendhal, Proust, and Dostoevsky, although he does distinguish between earlier and later developments in his myth of metaphysical desire in these novelists. Comparing *Don Quixote, The Red and the Black, The Remembrance of Things Past,* and *Notes from the Underground,* he finds that shifts in a succession of mediators appear and become more rapid, that progression toward the discovery of the absence of self and toward the discovery of artistic creation is more advanced. For Girard the *Recherche* is a novel of transcendence that goes beyond the struggles and frustration encountered in the movement toward a mediator. His study leaves us with a teleological view of the novel; in fact, for him, the Christian teleology of death, suffering, and redemption structures the novel. From this point of view, the initial frustration and death brought about by apparently outward searches for a supposed object (a woman, the aristocratic world) are properly understood only in juxtaposition to the final redemption or inner search for an imaginative synthesis of self and Other.

While Doubrovsky's careful analysis of Proust's unconscious voices within the specifically linguistic structures of the text enables him to differentiate between these structures and those that are the goal of the narrator, his analysis does not emphasize literary form to the extent that the text becomes static, as it does for Girard, Jeffrey Mehlman, and Gilles Deleuze. In his *Structural Study of Autobiography,* it may appear that Mehlman independently takes the same basic position—in the same year—as Doubrovsky. Yet for Mehlman the *Recherche* becomes a sequence of variations on the same model.[7] Like Doubrovsky, Mehlman demonstrates that

Proust recreates an original ambivalent relationship to the mother by attempting to establish an identity built upon an incestuous union. But although Mehlman suggests that unconscious desires are a source of discontinuity in an apparently coherent novel, his structural methodology leads him to describe the work as a series of repetitions of the bedtime scene. Unlike Doubrovsky, then, who studies changing unconscious desires, Mehlman studies a single unconscious structure underlying the narrative.

While temporal process seems to be crucial in Gilles Deleuze's complex structuralist interpretation of Proust, he does not actually read the text as if it exists from beginning to end in a process of becoming.[8] A contradiction emerges when we compare his theory and practice. Unlike Doubrovsky, for whom the unconscious relentlessly breaks through the conscious level of the novel, Deleuze studies the processes by which the former develops into the latter: in the course of the *Recherche*, the narrator gradually "deciphers signs"; that is, he becomes conscious of archetypal images within himself. The images that the narrator comes to perceive include those depicting society and love affairs in which change and wasted hours are experienced. A second group of images represents subjection to unavoidable change and to eventual death. In a third, a multiplicity of truths is perceived in "essences" of remembrance and art; in such essences, the encounter between subject and object produces a kind of new and unique world in which chronological time is transcended. These images or truths are understood as special effects brought about by a structure composed of three interacting levels corresponding to the three groups of images: lost time that fragments the experience of love and social climbing; lost time that brings inevitable change and death; and regained time that fuses a whole range of truths in privileged moments of artistic creativity.

For Deleuze, Proust creates a kind of literary machine that produces these privileged moments. The most important of these occur in the final episodes of the *Temps retrouvé*, where the narrator has an artistic vision that makes all signs intelligible. Deleuze reads the *Recherche* as a teleological system of signs finally and completely deciphered at the end of the novel. The steps leading to the end are relatively unimportant in this atemporal reading; Deleuze highlights instead the final experience in which past and present signs are simultaneously perceived and related.

Unlike that of Deleuze, Doubrovsky's analysis of the processes by which the psyche and its relationship to writing give rise to the *Recherche* emphasizes the dynamic quality of the novel. Differing too from more traditional versions of Freudian analysis of Proust, Doubrovsky does not see the text as a static representation of a neurotic complex.[9] Rather, he sees it as the genuine development of a neurosis: the narrator's attempts to reverse the original fantasy acted out in the madeleine episode generate the novel. Formerly dependent upon the mother and lacking an identity of his own, he "kills" her and creates a self in language. Throughout the *Place de la madeleine*, Doubrovsky demonstrates the various stages in this reversal of fantasy, as for instance in the description of Aunt Léonie (a transformation of the mother) and in the recurrent metaphor of the writer-mother who will "give birth" to the text.

As Doubrovsky has demonstrated, the transformations of the unconscious create an undeniably discontinuous structure in the *Recherche*, primarily because of the general reversal from dependent child to independent writer but also because of the ambivalent movements of the unconscious, both in relation to the mother and in relation to the text. Love for the mother constantly alternates with hate. After describing how the mother came to his bedside each night to kiss him (how love for the mother feeds his hunger for self), he describes how he managed to have her sleep by his bed for an entire night. Doubrovsky underlines the narrator's guilt (he feels he has caused her hair to begin to gray) and demonstrates that having her stay in the room is basically an aggressive act (punishment for her frequent withdrawals from him) in which he destroys her in order to attempt to create a sense of self. Desire to establish an identity in writing (the positive movement in the writer's relationship to the text) alternates with the desire to destroy the self that he creates in writing (the negative movement, motivated by the guilt he experiences for killing the mother). The narrator's ambivalent relationship to the quest for identity in his work is evident in the first-person perspective of the *Recherche*. The self whose life is related in the novel, beginning with the reconstruction of Combray and ending with the global memories of the *Temps retrouvé*, is referred to almost exclusively as a nameless "I" (or "me") and cannot be said to coincide with the author of the text, since this "I" possesses with certainty only a linguistic existence.

For Doubrovsky the stages of fantasy—that is, unconscious discourse in itself—constitute the primary source of change in Proust's novel. Occasionally, however, interaction between unconscious and conscious discourse is seen as a source of change. Doubrovsky demonstrates the way in which the madeleine scene may be understood as the most significant instance of a disruptive unconscious creating a gap in conscious narration. Without his psychoanalytic reading, which reveals the precise import of this scene, its relationship to the rest of the novel is an enigma. The episode is never clearly located in time (we are sure only that the narrator is an adult). The episode creates a gap between the short description of the bedtime scene in the chapter called "Overture" or "Combray I" and the greater part of the narrative in "Combray II," which emerges from the madeleine scene in an inexplicable way as a series of memories. The two portions of the novel remain distinct, separated by the mysterious taste of the tea and cake.

Despite differences between them, a comparison of Sartre and Doubrovsky is helpful in understanding the significance of Doubrovsky's approach. For Sartre in *Saint Genet*, as for the author of the *Madeleine*, the text is primarily temporal: consciousness exists in a state of flux and constantly alternates between the attempts (1) to make an object of itself and (2) to move beyond this object. In fact, Doubrovsky uses Sartrean vocabulary when he describes the literary work as a kind of spinning top or whirligig that never comes to a stop and turns from one alternative to its contrary. For both analysts the psyche, like the text in which it exists, has a mode of being that is discontinuous.

In light of the many atemporal readings of the novel, this discontinuous structure emerges both as Doubrovsky's most significant critical discovery and as a useful concept in the development of psychoanalytic criticism. At the level of unconscious desire, the writer's longing to construct a self, to be the mother, is constantly thwarted and constantly creates new fantasies of motherhood, the last of which is the fantasy of the writer. At the level of conscious reflection, the writer is continually frustrated in his persistent attempts to create an identifiable self. In the final pages of the *Recherche*, he writes knowing that he exists only as a series of different "someones" in his text. Doubrovsky underlines the way in which Proust questions writing as a construction of the self. Different from the many critics who confuse the theory of autobiographical fiction that the euphoric narrator discusses in the conclusion with the aesthetic of the entire *Recherche*, Doubrovsky (in part X) shows how Proust discovers the failure of the autobiographical narrative as an attempt to establish identity:

That the subject is "split open" by his discourse, that an absolute cleavage separates for him the order of Being and the order of the Logos, is neither Freud's "discovery" nor Lacan's but Proust's; his whole book consists in the setting in place of the transparent and unbridgeable distance that divides "I" as referent from "I" as reference, subject of existence ("hero") from subject of discourse ("Narrator"). It's a question here not of a temporal disjunction but of an ontological break.

Doubrovsky demonstrates, then, that Proust calls autobiographical writing into question and that Proust's project offers the model for the contemporary writer's project in general. Like all writing, the *Recherche* defines itself only, ultimately, to reject that definition.[10]

In its original lecture form, this study of the *Recherche* was delivered at the colloquium on Proust and the *nouvelle critique* at the Ecole Normale Supérieure in January 1972. William V. Spanos, editor of *Boundary 2*, sparked my interest in the *Place de la madeleine* when he asked me to translate for his journal the opening section of the book version of the lecture.

The first of many thorny problems posed by the translation was to determine the usual English equivalents for the French psycho-analytic terminology. James Strachey's translation of Freud in the *Standard Edition* and the translation of Laplanche's and Pontalis's *Dictionnaire de la psychanalyse, The Language of Psycho-analysis,* were particularly helpful in this regard.

A second difficulty concerned Doubrovsky's frequent use of puns in a discourse that is both precise and playful. Although I have been successful in retaining most of the word play or in creating compa-rable equivalents, there are a few exceptions. It is particularly un-fortunate that the puns on *propre*—meaning "clean," "proper," and "your own"—are lost in the translation, because the repeated use of *propre* lends a kind of unity to the original, and the meaning "your own" is of critical importance for Doubrovsky's thesis that the *Recherche* constitutes a frustrated quest for identity.

An early example of this loss appears on page 22. The pun re-surfaces in different forms in discussions of the creative writer who strives both to appropriate language and to achieve an impropriety of style, an individual style (*propriété,* p. 125; *impropre,* p. 128). A similar pun disappears in the translation of Doubrovsky's notion that "to find your own voice" (*trouver sa voie*) is at the same time "to find your own way" (*trouver sa voie,* p. 35).

Other lost puns include (1) *vouloir dire* (p. 29), "means" and "to want to say"—both translations are relevant to the discussion of the unconscious level of the text, where both desire and significa-tion are operative; (2) *fils* (p. 39), "threads" and "son," in the con-sideration of the masturbation scene in *Contre Sainte-Beuve,* where the creation of a web of words is likened to childbirth; (3) *Vivonne* (p. 49), "Vivonne river" and "life" (*vie*), in the examination of ways that Combray memories give rise to writing, a form of eternal life for an author; (4) *scène* (p. 80), "scene" and "Last Supper/ Holy Communion" (*cène*), in the analysis of the religious imagery Proust uses to describe art; (5) *jeu* (p. 98), "play" and "I" (*je*) in the discussion of the narrator's problematic identity and sexuality.

I would like to thank Marilyn Gaddis Rose, Serge Doubrovsky, and my husband Paul for their substantial help in preparing the translation. The editors of *Boundary 2* have kindly granted permission to publish the revised version of the first six sections, which originally appeared in that journal.

C. M. B.

Writing and Fantasy in Proust

I believe Proust has been overly aestheticized, asepticized. I would like to return his aggressive thrust to him, to restore his violence. His "Jeunes Filles en fleurs" are in effect "Fleurs du Mal."

With Proust you are weighed down by the criticism before you begin. To contribute to it, on a subject in appearance as rehashed as that of the famous *madeleine*, is in itself a rather serious decision. Yet nothing is less known than this passage too well known. You become ecstatic, instead of understanding. You repeat, after the author: involuntary memory versus voluntary memory. You celebrate the miracle of the Resurrection. Now we know—or we should know—that nothing is less innocent than memory. If it tells the truth, it's always with a lie. The madeleine experience, then, demands precisely the type of approach that has never been applied to it: a psychoanalytic investigation. I add immediately, of the *text*. I leave Proust and his catchall homosexuality to others. Like Freud approaching Jensen's *Gradiva*, we are approaching a book, and nothing else. It's more than enough.

Whenever in the system of conscious discourse an element of the discourse of the unconscious erupts, a comic effect is produced. This eruption takes place in the title of my book, *La Place de la madeleine*. A word play—not the importance or the meaning, but the *place*. Upon reflection, what had at first been for me an apparently innocuous and gratuitous joke turned out to generate the underlying meaning: the madeleine, the location of its being (where *its* place, the madeleine's, is); but there is also a reciprocal implication in my joke (where *my* place is, in the madeleine).

No need to linger over the obvious facts. Place of the madeleine: it's an *initial* experience. It opens the chapter "Combray II" and the *Recherche*, properly speaking. But it's also *initiative*. In the passage from voluntary to involuntary memory, the essential experience of the book is situated, the experience that produces the book. In a sense, then, it is *archetypal*. On the thematic level, it returns to obsess, to haunt the Narrator's life (1) in the series of explicit episodes of memory-jogging (court flagstones, fork noise, etc.) or of significant states of arousal, cut off from meaning (Martinville steeples, Hudimesnil trees); (2) in implicit visitations, such as the one in which the little phrase from the Vinteuil sonata torments Swann with its "exquisite and inexpressible pleasure," and also the "hawthorn" scene (I, 106) at one end of the olfactory scale, or that of the "lavatory" (I, 376) at the other: the enigma of a sensorial cipher to be solved.[1] Structurally, it can be said that the madeleine episode serves as a model for the whole of the *Recherche*, to the extent that (borrowing Deleuze's schema) it is the totality of the book that presents itself (a) as a deciphering, (b) as an apprenticeship of signs.

Now what is the place of this experience, a constituent element of the themes and structure, in the narrative chain? The Narrator says that it is a kind of matrix: "the whole of Combray and of its surroundings, taking their proper shapes and growing solid, sprang into being, town and gardens alike, from my cup of tea" (I, 36). Criticism has generally followed suit. There is *voluntary* memory, which reveals Combray I (the bedtime scene in the Overture) only, and *involuntary* memory, from which Combray II emerges, the "true" one, restored in its integrity, "finally, as it exists in itself." A lovely scheme, wrong only in that it is too simple. Initial, initiative, central, archetypal—the madeleine experience is, in a manner which is at the very least curious, narratively *unplaceable*. It is easily locatable on the level of the articulation itself, since it gives rise to the story; on the level of what is articulated, however (its place in the story), the experience is unplaceable; the tracks become confused.

In his very precise study of narrative voice in the *Recherche*, Marcel Muller tries in vain to situate with precision the Subject's position in his own story.[2] The Subject who relives the nightly bedtime drama has already sojourned at Tansonville (I, 6); he has not yet experienced the madeleine revelation. Has the Subject who evokes Swann's love had this experience or not? *Noms de Pays: le Nom* poses the same problem. At the moment when Muller thinks that he has resolved the problem (the episode probably takes place during the Narrator's sojourn "far from Paris . . . in a sanitarium"; II, 892), he proclaims the fragility of his own hypothesis in a note: "The mother's presence and the fact that the 'I' is at home at this time obviously contradict the hypothesis according to which the reign of the Subject coincides with the period of the sojourn in the nursing home" (Muller, 44). Whether or not one may respond: "Yes, but nothing prevents the Narrator from returning home on one occasion" matters little. The important point (and I refer here to Muller's fascinating diagram) is that, except for the narrative syntagma Madeleine–Combray II, it is in practical terms very difficult to situate the other passages of the *Recherche* in relation to the madeleine episode (before or after?).

Looking closely, we see something even stranger. The Narrator seems to describe the madeleine experience as if it had enabled him to see again something which, without it, would have remained invisible—in short, as the equivalent of an anamnesis. But it's only make-believe, an "as if." The Narrator sees again only "the bare minimum of scenery necessary . . . as though all Combray had consisted of but two floors joined by a slender staircase, and as though there had been no time there but seven o'clock at night" (I, 33). Now the text that immediately precedes the madeleine scene is completely explicit on this point:

I must own that I could have assured any questioner that Combray did include other scenes and did exist at other hours than these. But since the facts which I should then have recalled would have been prompted only by an exercise of the will, by my intellectual memory, and since the pictures which that kind of memory shows us of the past preserve nothing of the past itself, I should never have had any wish to ponder over this residue of Combray. [1, 33]

Contrary to the accepted interpretation, the Narrator does not tell us that the difference between the first Combray "apparition" and the second would be one of remembrance, the Combray II evocations (church, streets, houses, etc.) remaining inaccessible to him. He does not say that without the madeleine experience he *could* not have thought of it (a curious case of amnesia would be necessary for that), but that he would not have "wished" to think of it. What we see here, then, is not a kind of abrupt genesis—unexpected emergence of what is hidden, resurrection of the lost memory—but reanimation of what is known, reactivation of what is banal. In a word, what is new here is not the representation, the images themselves, but the affective thrust with which they suddenly become charged. We must not fear having the Narrator contradict himself in this regard. When he says, "Seek? More than that: create," he attributes to the "visual memory" which is evidently *given* to him ("And suddenly the memory returns"; 1, 36) the creative force that belongs only to *metaphorical writing*, transforming rudimentary recollection into narrative: "just as the Japanese amuse themselves by filling a porcelain bowl with water and steeping in it little crumbs of paper which until then . . . without character or form . . . become flowers or houses or people, permanent and recognisable" (1, 36).

Inasmuch as metaphors have already been widely discussed, I think the principle Proust is emphasizing here is that *what sets writing [écriture] in motion is what moves it.* The enigma, let us recall, is not resolved in an instant with the final connection of the "visual memory," disarming in its very banality (Aunt Léonie's teas), and the cup's present "taste." The completely filled memory gap neither removes nor yields the experience's secret. The question is the violent and strange nature of an affect: "an exquisite pleasure . . . detached, with no suggestion of its origin," preceding the act of memory and surviving it: "I had ceased now to feel mediocre, accidental, mortal" (I, 34). It is this ultimate deciphering, absent from the text, that I would like to attempt here and that invites us all the more if we recall that to escape mediocrity, contingency, and death defines the very meaning of the act of writing for Proust.

◀ 2 ▶

A make-believe anamnesis, we were saying—but too quickly. The mental operation described by Proust with clinical precision is indeed the homologue of the act of recollection in analysis: a patient and obstinate quest for sensory associations, having as its object the "final enlightenment" (I, 34). A scene endlessly sketched and avoided: "I retrace my thoughts," "I find again the same state," "feeling that my mind is growing fatigued without having any success." Repression, resistance, it's all there—"I shut out every obstacle," "I can measure the resistance"—with, in the end, success: "And suddenly the memory returns."

What is deceptive here is not the process of anamnesis but the object at which it becomes arrested. Because, to take up what we were just saying, if the madeleine episode does not give rise to Combray at the narrative level, if its place is at once precisely locatable (in the articulation itself) and lost (in the story that is articulated), it is because the memory in question is a screen-memory. We find there the classic contrast between the clarity, the exceptional insistence of representations, and the lack of interest, the *innocence* of manifest content. More exactly, if screen-memories, according to Freud's formula, "represent childhood's forgotten years as faithfully as manifest content represents its thoughts," and if what is forgotten in this case is none other than the child's sexual experiences and fantasies, we may then wonder *what*, in the madeleine experience, the recovered memory *screens*. Not what is clearly presented, but what is coated over and elusive.

The psychological method, dear to Mauron, of superimposing

texts, may provide a preliminary answer. And here I would like to take the opportunity to mention Philippe Lejeune's remarkable article, "Ecriture et sexualité," published in a special issue of the journal *Europe* (1971).[3] In a fine analysis, also dedicated to the "madeleine," which at many points converges with and at others diverges from my own, Lejeune is to my knowledge the first to indicate the astonishing textual corroboration between the youthful masturbation description in the *Contre Sainte-Beuve* (p. 30)[4] and the madeleine experience in the *Recherche:*

Then, in search of a pleasure that I did not know, I began to explore myself. [CSB]
An exquisite pleasure had invaded my senses, but individual, detached, with no suggestion of its origin. [Recherche]
My consciousness, exalted by pleasure, knew itself to be wider and more powerful than the universe which I saw remotely through the window. [CSB]
All this world reposed on me, and I was more than it, and could not die. [CSB]
It is time to stop; the potion is losing its magic. It is plain that the object of my quest, the truth, lies not in the cup but in myself. [Recherche]
This essence was not in me, it was myself. I had ceased to feel mediocre, accidental, mortal. Whence could it have come to me, this all-powerful joy? [Recherche]

The masturbation experience from the earlier text very clearly underlies that of the madeleine in the *Recherche*, producing the same series of effects: (1) the feeling, founded upon the discovery of ipseity, that thought is omnipotent; (2) superiority over the exterior world, transcendence of contingency; (3) intense joy, deliverance from death.

The masturbation experience itself is not simple. Proust, in the *Contre Sainte-Beuve*, distinguishes substitutive or secondary masturbation (in place of an absent sexual object) and what I will call primary masturbation, pleasure that is "not a substitute for anything else" (quest for personal identity, enjoyment of "personality"; CSB, 30, 31). It does not seem farfetched to relate this clear-sighted distinction to the Freudian concepts of secondary narcissism (the turning back upon the ego of the libido, withdrawn from object-cathexis; *An Outline of Psychoanalysis*) and primary narcissism (the total investment of the child's libido in himself: the child takes himself as a love object, this state corresponding to the child's belief in the omnipotence of his thoughts; *Totem and Taboo*).

The superimposition of Proustian and Freudian texts may be fruitfully added to the superimposition of Proustian texts among themselves. The transformation of the *Contre Sainte-Beuve* and *Recherche* experiences seems, then, to function according to the following model: the madeleine experience replaces that of *primary masturbation*, the *Recherche* text retaining only the "substitutive" masturbation, which is unessential (I, 121); concurrently, from the first to the second text, the memory experience is transformed. In the *Contre Sainte-Beuve* the sensation of a slice of "dry toast" or "rusk," dunked in tea, *immediately* gives rise to the series of childhood memories (CSB, 20), but without any cosmic significance, any feeling of immortality; in contrast, the recollection experience in the *Recherche* becomes charged with the *delays* of the masturbatory act whose stages it repeats ("feeling that my mind is growing fatigued without having any success to report, I compel it for a change to enjoy that distraction. . . . And then for a second time, I clear an empty space in front of it. . . . Ten times over I must essay the task. . . . And suddenly the memory returns"; I, 35–36), and reproduces the concomitant consciousness of omnipotence and of triumph over death. Furthermore, there is, in the form of a final metaphor (which to say the least is incongruous), a *textual* trace of this transformation of masturbation into memory storage at the very end of the passage where smell and taste, last survivors from the past, remain "and bear unfaltering, in the tiny and almost impalpable *drop* of their essence, the vast structure of recollection" (I, 36).

In conclusion, at the end of a first series of substitutive transformations, the passage from masturbation to memory—with the displacement of the jubilant affect from one experience to the other—produces the change from "dry toast" to "madeleine," whose place we can perhaps now pinpoint more easily.

◀ 3 ▶

For all that, however, do we have the answer to our first question: if the memory induced by the madeleine experience is a screen-memory, and if this same experience is presented as a translation or transference of a masturbatory experience, can we conclude that what the remembrance screens is masturbation? Why such a displacement? Why would the masturbatory act alone be the object of a curious censorship, whereas other "depraved" scenes are detailed for us in the *Recherche* (tribadism, sodomization, profanation, Charlus's brothel, and the like). Besides, this censorship does not exist. The Narrator, if I may say so, masturbates, but "secondarily" (I, 121). The problem, then, is not, what does Proust hide from us (he hides nothing from us, and especially not an already minutely described onanism scene), but what does he hide from *himself?* More precisely, what does he hide from himself concerning the solitary practices he evokes? The answer is in no way doubtful. He conceals from himself their *meaning*. And it is this repressed meaning which, from one text to the other, produces—by a double process of displacement and condensation, on the psychic level, metonymnically and metaphorically, from the point of view of writing—the celebrated *madeleine*.

Displacement: *what place change?* Metonymy: in the narrative chain, *the madeleine is where?* Notice that the masturbation scene (which it replaces) is, in the *Contre Sainte-Beuve* (whatever "order" we assume in the latter), anywhere, that is, nowhere. It's an important or fascinating scene among others, a "link" in the narrative chain. Held within the structure of the narrative, it has no hold over its structure. It has been known for a long time that it's the reverse in the *Recherche*. The madeleine functions as matrix of the narrative. The suddenly retrieved memory *generates* the narrative, *engenders* the book. Before: Combray I (empty memories revolving around the "bedtime scene," a "luminous panel, sharply defined

"À la Recherche d'une Lentille de Contact," d'après Millet.

the ce
Party's
mous
McG
ated m
ocrats
has be

Th
has at
priety.
istratic
tions t
labor u
court-
of wro
that he
becom
1994.
White
ter sca
merou
mony
the Se
sible p
Benne
"cheap
numbe

"Nah, I didn't watch the Olympics—who won?"

MANKOFF

•

•

1964, he attended a talk about the civil-rights movement given by Allard Lowenstein, an assistant dean who was already a kind of Pied Piper of youth activism in America. Ickes became a civil-rights vol-

During the seventies, he was diagnosed as a narcoleptic and given massive prescription doses of Dexedrine, an amphetamine. Although he says he is no longer taking the drug, he still has chronic in-

against a vague and shadowy background"; I, 33). After: Combray
II and everything that follows (memory unfolding according to a
temporal order and a spatial organization that are complex but
relatively stable memorial blocks, which illuminate each other in
turn). To use a rather rough formula, we might say: without the
madeleine, no *Recherche*.

But what does this mean? And how does this sudden recollection
set the text in motion—not by restoring, as we have seen, but by
reinvesting accessible but "dead" memories? The text answers:
"The whole of Combray and of its surroundings, taking their proper
shapes and growing solid, sprang into being, town and gardens
alike, from my cup of tea" (I, 36). The madeleine experience gives
shape and *solidity*. (From a thematic point of view, notice the insistence of the "stony" element in the descriptions of the church, the
streets, the houses, at the beginning of Combray II.) Shape and
solidity to what? Obviously, to what is formless and hazy. The re-
surgence of the affect organizes and structures the floating signifier
"Combray."

We can put the question again in a different way. What lacks solidity and shape *before* the madeleine experience? "When I awoke
like this, and my mind struggled in an unsuccessful attempt to discover where I was, everything would be moving round me through
the darkness: things, places, years" (I, 5). Combray I, which opens
upon the scene of insomniac awakening and closes upon the neurotic bedtime scene, poses, in connection with the empirical problem of sleep, the ontological problem of the identity of being—
more exactly, of ipseity: "When I awoke at midnight, not knowing
where I was, I could not be sure at first who I was" (I, 5). To pass
from the "sense of existence, such as may lurk and flicker in the
depths of an animal's consciousness" to a self that is human or even
hominid ("I was more destitute of human qualities than the cave-
dweller"; I, 5), nothing less than memory is necessary—more precisely, the *memory of places*, whose function as a constitutive element of the self is underlined from the word go, and well before the
madeleine experience (which is only a special case of it): "The
memory, not yet of the place in which I was, but of various other

places where I had lived, and might now very possibly be, would come . . . to draw me up out of the abyss of not-being, from which I could never have escaped by myself" (I, 5). In the opposite direction, all Combray "sprang into being, town and gardens alike, from my cup of tea." By the mediation of places, what is taking "proper shape" and "growing solid," is *the Narrator's self*, lost at the beginning of Combray I, retrieved with Combray II.

A rigorously parallel operation is in question. If Golo's magic lantern creates a "malaise" by projecting (if we may say so) the experience of the imaginary or of non-being "into a room which I had succeeded in filling with my own personality" (I, 8), in the madeleine experience the sudden filling of the self with the unknown pleasure ("the vicissitudes of life had become indifferent to me . . . filling me with a precious essence; or rather this essence was not in me, it was myself"; I, 34), that is, ultimately, the filling of the self with its own *self essence*, will brusquely project not "the whole of Combray" but a *room:* "And suddenly the memory returns. The taste was that of the little crumb of madeleine which on Sunday mornings at Combray . . . when I went to say good day to her in her bedroom, my Aunt Léonie used to give me" (I, 36).

If I take up again my question—the madeleine gives shape and solidity to *what?*—the answer becomes: to the Narrator's *self*, by instituting a curious system of filling and emptying in relation to a *room.* The question now becomes in turn: what is it, then, that differentiates this relation in Combray I and Combray II—more exactly, what happens in the madeleine experience to reverse it? The operation of this system must undoubtedly be examined with more precision. The internal relationship of the self to the room in which it lives passes through the intermediary of the *bed.* The Proustian place par excellence (of love, of dream, of sleep, of insomnia, of reclusion, of sickness, of death, of reading, and finally of writing), the bed in Combray I is above all marked by an essential ambivalence. Experienced as a "nest" where "I would . . . bury my head" (I, 6), "a cave of warmth dug out of the heart of the room itself," the pleasure "of being shut in from the outer world" (I, 6), the bed is a place of plenitude—only to become, immediately thereafter, a "monstrous funnel" where you suffer (I, 7), a sepulcher where you "bury yourself," a "grave" which you yourself must dig (I, 22), an experience of this "not-being" out of which only memory can pull you. This reversal from emptiness to fullness and from fullness to emptiness gives structure or, better, rhythm to the surface sequences of the narrative at an archaic level where we may already recognize the Freudian *Fort-Da* of *Beyond the Pleasure Principle*. The narrative itself, as a whole, operates within this underlying system. Indeed, both

COMBRAY I
And so it was that, for a long time afterwards, when I lay awake at night and revived old memories of Combray, I saw no more of it than this sort of luminous panel (I, 33)

and

COMBRAY II
And so I would often lie until morning, dreaming of the old days at Combray, of my melancholy and wakeful evenings there; of other days besides, the memory of which had been more lately restored to me by the taste . . . of a cup of tea (I, 143)

are inscribed, including the madeleine, in what we might call the insomnia structure. In both cases, in a bed in which being's presence/absence to itself confront each other, it is a question of "filling" the vacuity of a faltering self with the memories that restore its substance. Narrative microstructures reproduce the text's global structure. As early as Combray I, two important sequences are articulated in this way. First, *the Golo episode* (I, 8): room (full: "which I had succeeded in filling with my own personality") → magic lantern (empty: derealization through the experience of the imaginary) → "malaise" → "I would run down to the dining-room" → Françoise's *boeuf à la casserole* and "fall into the arms of my mother." The problematic of mental plenitude refers back to the primitive model of physical repletion: *food* + *mother*, mediated in the nineteenth-century bourgeoisie by the *cook*.

In a different way, the *bedtime scene* (I, 21ff.) is constructed ac-

cording to the same schema: bed (empty: "dig my own grave") →
"agony" → calls "Françoise, my aunt's cook" → to obtain the "food" of
a maternal kiss (full: mother's presence). The "food of a kiss" that
closes Combray I is, however, given only in the form of a lack:
"brief and stealthy" (I, 21); "such a night could not be repeated"
(I, 33). It is the exception that confirms the rule of abstinence
("this new kindness that my childhood had not known"; I, 30). In
terms of maternal nourishment, it is clear that the child of Combray I remains hungry. Precisely this same hunger, as a matter of
fact, will produce the madeleine. Metonymically, in the narrative
chain, it is produced *at the place where* we might say that the text
comes to an end for lack of substance (emptiness of the insomniac
being who is incapable of filling himself all alone), as we say that
combat ceases for lack of combatants. Metaphorically, in the system of fantasies, the madeleine is produced *in place of* the childhood nourishment that was lacking. The Narrator takes his fill in
order to make up for the lack. Such is, I believe, *the place* of the
madeleine. We are now, no doubt, less surprised that the "exquisite
pleasure" which accompanies the eating of it resembles "the effect
which love has" (I, 34).

◄ 4 ►

"Exquisite pleasure." Certainly. But "detached, with no suggestion
of its cause." The madeleine's place is clearly that of a tenacious
repression. And in bringing its "detachment" to a halt—that is, by
connecting it to the rest of our analysis—we must at least try to
give some suggestion of this "cause," which the Narrator, even after
the emergence of the memory, leaves unexplained.

What does the Narrator hide, not from *us* but from *himself*, we
were asking earlier, in connection with the onanistic practices that
the madeleine experience pretends to screen. He hides their meaning, we were saying—a meaning made occult by a process that
"would produce," from the point of view of the text as well as of
fantasy, the "madeleine." It is time to attack the semantic problem
directly at the level of metaphorical substitutions, if it is true, ac-

cording to our analysis, that the madeleine's *place* is to be *in place of*. Must we translate: *in place of the mother?*

Here we pick up Philippe Lejeune's penetrating analysis in the previously cited article: "The substitution of the madeleine for the dry toast served to represent in an obscure way the reminiscence's fundamental object: the mother" (p. 120). Form (female sex); name (the evangelic sinner's first name, sensuality and culpability cycle, resurrection myth, which govern the system of the *Recherche*); taste (infusion and madeleine replacing bread and wine in a rite of "oral communion with the mother"). After a long detour along the path of Proust's homosexuality, on which we will not follow him, Lejeune concludes that, masturbation being "the form which the relationship with the mother takes at the time of puberty" (p. 140), the ultimate object of the reminiscence is—by way of the image of the *Jet d'eau* in Hubert Robert's painting evoked in the *Contre Sainte-Beuve*—"this central presence of orgasm" (p. 141), "this totalizing function of masturbation and of orgasm in the underlying architecture of the work" (p. 142). In short, we might say that owing to the relation masturbation/mother, by a kind of shift a euphoriant oral regression (perceptible in all of "Combray") masks orgasmic enjoyment, object of the forbidden pleasure, by covering it over with precision. From this perspective, the object of the reminiscence would be displaced from the madeleine to the mother, and from the mother to masturbation.

This analysis, which should be followed in detail, appears accurate overall, provided that it be substantially modified—less in its approach and results than in what I am inclined to call its hermeneutic "accent." The explicator, who discovers only positivity in "communion" with the mother or the bursting forth of orgasm, seems to be caught up in the Narrator's "Combraysian" euphoria. At the end of these explanations, we see little reason for the repression or, if we prefer, for the disguise of the masturbatory scene. From a psychoanalytic perspective more than any other, Valéry's adage is called for: "But to reflect the light / Bespeaks another half of mournful shade." It's a matter of restoring this "half of mournful shade," the analytic task being always, and by definition, thankless. Clearly we find here the lineaments of an answer to the question posed at the very beginning: what is *my* place, in the madeleine? Carried by the text, which brings me forth as a critic, I turn back *against it* the aggression *for the mother* that is hidden there. All filiation relationships being a struggle for mastery, conquest of an in-dependence, the ultimate cipher of the "madeleine" is clearly a metaphor for my own deciphering. In this way, the Proustian wish that every reader be the reader of himself is fulfilled.

It's a lovely fairy tale that Proust tells us in Combray, and Lejeune following Proust. Indeed, if the Proustian Narrator, without our even leaving "Swann's way" for the tortuous paths of *La Prisonnière*, is evidently the epitome of the obsessional neurotic (so much so that at times it seems Freud was thinking of him in writing *The Rat Man*), where, then, in this edifying story has the ambivalence conflict gone? It is passed over in silence, a fact which, of itself, explicitly indicates the place of the repression—the (metaphorical) place of the madeleine. The madeleine is first of all a madeleine—I mean a cake, a treat. Let's keep from making it immediately burst into symbolic series; let's instead respect the signifier's insistence. The madeleine *is something to eat*, as it literally appears in the narrated and recollected scenes, so much so that even psychic acts are evoked in the form of mastication—his "laziness" prompting the Narrator to turn away from the difficult experience taking place to think of his "hopes for tomorrow, which let themselves be pondered over [*remâcher*, literally, "ruminated"] without effort or distress of mind" (1, 35). The madeleine, however, *is ruminated* (remembered) *with effort and distress*. Why? If I refer here to my preceding analysis, Combray 1 closes upon the obsession with an unsatisfied "need to eat" (Françoise's *boeuf à la casserole* or Mamma's kiss functioning as stopgaps for a lack). The madeleine is, then, fantasized here not in place of the mother in general but, more precisely, in place of maternal nourishment that was lacking—an absent place indicated in the Narrator's later behavior, his refusal to touch madeleines: "I had so often seen such things in the interval, *without tasting them*, on the trays in pastry-cooks' windows" (1, 36). The transgression of what he himself had forbidden undoubtedly explains the violence of the affective discharge when he suddenly *eats them again.*

The transgression is not performed, however, without resistance on the Subject's part. Let us reread the beginning of the scene: "My mother, seeing that I was cold, offered me some tea, *a thing I did not ordinarily take. I declined* at first, and then, for no particular reason, *changed my mind*" (I, 34). Here we get a glimpse of the essential conflict of familial parent-child relationships of force, according to the ternary structure order/refusal/obedience, with, of course, the concomitant repression of hostility ("for no particular reason, changed my mind"). Notice the fundamental role of habit in the Proustian universe; a change is all the more cause for arousal because it is a question of a radical reversal. The madeleine scene (which immediately follows it in the narrative) exactly *reverses* the scene of the mother's kiss (introducing, in order to do this, the maternal actant in the *Recherche*, whereas the tea, in the *Contre Sainte-Beuve*, had been given by an "old cook"): just as the child had forced his mother *against her custom* to retire near him, his mother obliges the Narrator *against his custom* to drink tea. The cup of tea is the mother's revenge, punishment for the wrong he is conscious of having done her.

Even more exactly, the scene of filial abdication corresponds to that of a maternal "abdication." But, one may say, offering tea and compelling the violation of a nighttime regulation are incommensurable acts. Indeed, they are two different stage effects or games in which the stakes remain identical; in both cases, it is a question of *sleeping*. By not coming to kiss him, the mother condemns the child to an insomniac wait. He will find sleep only by getting the better of her. Inversely, in order to get the better of him, she will want to deprive him of it: hence the gift of tea—"a thing I never drink"—is specified (CSB, 19) and with good reason, because tea, like coffee, which is often mentioned in the *Recherche*, is a fatal stimulant. As a matter of fact, it is not only mothers but lovers who begrudge you your sleep: at a romantic tea party at the Swanns', "Gilberte was making 'my' tea. I went on drinking it indefinitely, whereas *a single cup would keep me awake for twenty-four hours*"

(I, 378). It is understood that since a mother does not possess the immediate seduction of a sexual object, the Narrator—who lets himself be led by Gilberte—at first resists the poisonous maternal gift.

It is, in fact, precisely here that the first appearance of the madeleine is found. In order to surmount the aversion to her harmful philter, the mother appeals to the gourmand in her son: "She sent out for one of those short, plump little cakes called 'petites madeleines,' which look as though they had been moulded in the fluted scallop of a pilgrim's shell" (I, 34). And undoubtedly, in order to arrive at the maternal fantasy fixation in the madeleine, not only on the metonymic level (she sends for it) but also on the metaphoric (it is she), we should bring into play the symbolic associations that Philippe Lejeune's fine article reveals: cake in the shape of the female sexual organ; value of the "name" ("Madeleine complex"). According to the terms of our own analysis, the pastry as a matter of fact *fills* ("moulded in the . . . shell") the bed's *hollow* ("monstrous funnel"), the memory's *gaps*, which caused the Narrator's anguish in Combray I.

Perhaps we may now better grasp the meaning of the cup of tea, or what is at stake in the *insomnia*. If, as we have seen, the latter constitutes vacillation of the self, identity vertigo, experience of the nothingness from which only material memories release us, the offer of maternal nourishment provides the answer: "You are what I give you." (Lejeune has quite rightly observed that of all the reminiscence episodes—court flagstones, spoon that jingles, etc.—the episide of the madeleine is the only one where the object that arouses the reminiscence is "*given* by someone to the Narrator"). Moreover, rather than "offer," we should say "offering"; the "ritual" dinners of Combray are an offertory. You dedicate yourself to the family god. "Petites Madeleines," with capitals, which are incongruous for such ordinary cakes; "coquille de Saint-Jacques" (scallop shell):[5] associations with religious value, by which the meal is transformed into a cult celebrated time and again at Combray—cult of the mother or of maternal figures (Françoise, Aunt Léonie, the grandmother, the great-aunts).

The quest for *identity* unites, in a single narrative network, Combray I and Combray II, sleeping and eating. With the madeleine, the mother lets the son have it—she strikes him with "ontological nourishment": "I stuff you, I occupy your empty (insomniac) moments, I fill you with being." In fact, upon eating the madeleine, he is overjoyed. The Combraysian paradise soon emerges. "An exquisite pleasure had invaded my senses." Exactly, provided that it be "detached, with no suggestion of its origin." It is here that the repression takes effect: "This essence was not in me; it was myself." The truth reveals itself in the form of the *denial*; it is precisely the *opposite* which must be read: "This essence was not myself; it was in me." His essence is placed *in him* by the mother. She gives or withdraws insomnia/vertigo, food/identity. Withdrawn ("the object of my quest, the truth, lies not in the cup but in myself"), the Narrator discovers that, in his "self," there is the Other. He has, then, been robbed of himself. Now, he is so well "filled" by the madeleine—by all of Combray's food—that, as we so rightly say, "he has no more room" (*il n'a pas de place*). The madeleine's place is *there*, is *that*: the Narrator's place in which the madeleine "moulds itself" so well that it *takes* this place.

Rite and rhythm of meals: "reading until the good dinner which Françoise was preparing" (I, 66); "I say, an hour-and-a-half still before luncheon" (I, 85). Seasonal procession of dishes; obsession with those "Proustian foods" well examined by J.-P. Richard. In the Combraysian universe, abundance is superabundance. Eating is overeating. Aunt Léonie's bedrooms become, as soon as they are evoked, a "country cake," an "immense puff-pastry" (I, 38), whose essential form is *puffiness* ("the fire, baking like a pie the appetising smells . . . puffed them and glazed them and fluted them and swelled them" I, 38). You don't have to be a genius to see that an excess indicates an insatiable lack; if the madeleine's "exquisite pleasure" resembles "the effect which love has" (I, 34), the madeleine of course is not *love*; it is the lack of it. The madeleine's place: it satisfies *in place of*. It is the masking of a lack.

Upon close reading, moreover, this is visible in the narrative. Clearly, if the Narrator is cold, what should warm him is the *tea*, which he resists for the reasons considered. The madeleine serves, if I may say so, to "sugarcoat the pill," to make the tea acceptable, as castor oil is sweetened ("I raised to my lips a spoonful of the tea in which I had soaked a morsel of the cake"). The madeleine is swallowed immediately, then it is a question only of the "magic potion" and its successive "mouthfuls." In a sense, the true maternal substance is the fatal *tea*. By offering him a cup, under the euphoriant disguise of the madeleine, the mother wants (1) to prevent him from being himself (the vacillation and loss of self in insomnia); (2) to force him to be himself (to release himself on his own from nothingness, to subsist through his own means). In both cases, she forces him to *be without her*.

Now—such is the nodal point of his neurosis—this is precisely what the Narrator *wants* and *does not* want, or *wants* most and *can do* least. On a single page, he defines his "disordered nerves" as "a tendency to melancholy, to *solitude*" (I, 55), but declares a few lines later to his mother/grandmother: "I shouldn't be able to live *without you*." This childhood conflict echoes its contradiction at all levels of his behavior: loving "solitude," he is "worldly" and "snobbish," the most gregarious of creatures; distrusting friendship and love (Saint-Loup, Albertine) as a turning away from the self, an unbearable alienation, when he finds himself truly alone (unfamiliar room at Balbec), he cries: "I was utterly alone: I longed to die" (I, 507).

The contradiction is insoluble and the disorder incurable. If Proustian desire is *the madeleine (mother) must satisfy the lack (of love)*, he is doomed to failure, however he applies himself. As a matter of fact, in one way the demand is insatiable: *there is never enough love*. The meaning of the "oral" regression represented by the madeleine scene, in relation to that of adolescent masturbation—which it replaces—in the earlier text ("when I was twelve years old"; CSB, 30), resides in the fact that it refers back from a kind of "genital" love to an archaic *love model* of a nutritive type: kissing his grandmother at Balbec, "when I felt my mouth glued to her cheeks, to her brow, I drew from them something so beneficial, so *nourishing* that I lay in her arms as motionless, as solemn, as calmly gluttonous as a *babe at the breast*" (I, 50). (I should mention here that a study of the Narrator's sexuality would show two constant characteristics: first, erotic fixation on the "cheek," whatever the object—mother, Gilberte, Albertine; second, a striking series of "milkmaids," who pass through the *Recherche* from one end to the other and whom the Narrator desires, but who are "little girls," the genital possession of whom is forbidden.) Being loved, for the Proustian self, is being constantly "filled" by the "nutritious" presence of the maternal "Other"—a more thorough analysis would have to distinguish the different instances of the maternal imago, the cleavage mother/grandmother and the triad mother/grandmother/Aunt Léonie being essential. This filling up is, however, impossible, since in order that something not be lacking in this love *at every moment*, you must have *everything:* "Love, in the painful anxiety as in the blissful desire is the insistence upon a whole" (II, 453).

As early as Combray I, the structure of celebrated Proustian "jealousy" is in place. He can never have the *totality of his mother* as his own. There are "those inaccessible and torturing hours into which she had gone to taste of unknown pleasures" (I, 24); in particular, let us not forget that the "bedtime scene" is linked to the "dinner scene," where his mother is precisely in the process of feeding someone other than *soi* (himself): *Swann*, tormenting, phonetic twinning, which survives the elimination of Jean Santeuil's—and Marcel Proust's—"brother." His mother cannot be completely possessed; robbed of love by his (real or symbolic) father and brother, she can feed the child only intermittently. Her presence/absence gives rhythm to the fullness/emptiness of the vital flux, determines the sequences ecstasy/anguish, repletion/depression pinpointed in Combray I and infinitely repeated in the Narrator's life. There is no mode of existence other than this legacy of early childhood. In his system of defenses, the celebrated "heart's intermissions" revealed later (which concern precisely the death of the mother/grandmother against whom they turn) simply echo that law of existence to which a much more distant intermission has subjected him.

It is interesting to note the extent to which Marcel's and Albertine's relationship is an untiringly faithful replay of that of the Narrator and his mother. "Grown up," this time, he himself is his mother: "Asleep, awake, I should find her again this evening, when I chose to return home, Albertine, my little child" (ii, 556). Watch, sleep, bedroom, bed: in identical settings, he takes up the same scenes, this time with Albertine in his own role. He himself makes her eat (fundamental importance of food in their relations; ii, 467ff.); he himself watches her sleep (Albertine's "calm slumber delighted me, as a mother is delighted . . . by the sound sleep of her child"; ii, 459). Old fantasy acted out, ancient revenge: this time, he holds the woman/child "captive." She exists only to satisfy his every whim, to obey his every desire; she lives only to make him completely happy. Now, he is the master. "I was more of a master than I had supposed. More of a master, in other words more of a slave" (ii, 488). He wants the adult's omnipotence but conceives of only juvenile enjoyment. He must, then, become a mother while, however, remaining a child. Hardly grown, he regresses. Same settings, same scenes; he takes up his role. He reenlists. Bedroom: he will be the recluse. Bed: he will be the imaginary invalid ("I told her that the doctor had ordered me to stay in bed. This was not true"; ii, 394). Kiss: "to keep Albertine by my bedside, at once as a mistress, a sister, a daughter; *as a mother too*, of whose regular goodnight kiss I was beginning again to feel the childish need" (ii, 456).

Having looped the loop, we are back in Combray i, but it's more perfect, more subtle. Roles are double. If, in order to master the need for love, the Scene of Scenes must be recreated—the alternation, loved and hated, of the childhood *Fort-Da*—Marcel fabricates from now on the carefully regulated departures/returns of a child/mother, of whom he will be the master/slave. He will have Albertine read to him, as his mother had him do; at the same time, he will teach Albertine to read, as he had "to teach" his mother the true value of George Sand (i, 32). At once adult/child, he is torturer/victim, if it is true that according to his own definition, "I here give the name of love to a mutual torment" (ii, 455).

What is true of love for the Other is also true of love for oneself—doubly tormenting. Because if, as we have just seen, *there is never enough* love to satisfy the demand (just as there is never enough truth to fill "the great white gaps" of lies and false pretenses, since love and truth must, by virtue of a similar logic, be total in order to be), from another perspective, the opposite may be said. *There is always too much* love. Insoluble contradiction, which constitutes the knot of the essential conflict in which the Narrator struggles like someone tied up. In the exact proportion to which he needs to be "fed" by the Other, this alienating food is what prevents him from being himself—the ultimate goal of the *Recherche*. (Desired) repletion changes into (detested) repression. A remarkable sentence from *La Prisonnière* summarizes this fatal dialectic:

Whereupon, a famished convalescent who has already begun to batten upon all the desires that are still forbidden him, I asked myself whether marriage with Albertine would not spoil my life, as well by making me assume the burden, too heavy for my shoulders, of consecrating myself to another person, as by forcing me to live in absence from myself because of her continual presence and depriving me, forever, of the delights of solitude. [II, 396]

"Hunger" for all the "foods" that are lacking and will always be lacking arouses the demand for a "continual presence" of the nutritious Other, which, in return, gives rise to a permanent "absence from himself." Proustian hell may be expressed in a short formula: need for the love of the Other, whom one is incapable of loving, by which the very thing that fills the self is that which expels it.

The "full" self, stuffed with its own substance, of which the Narrator dreams is a pure mirage. Because if he refuses to "consecrate" himself "to another person" (this is the beginning of autonomy), he demands that another being devote herself to him (this is the end of it). In any case, *in terms of his being, he depends upon the Other*—the Narrator's obsessive "snobbism" demonstrates this ultimate truth in its social caricature. If being a "snob" is to desire what others desire, *with regard to his desire, he depends upon the Other*. This fundamental lack of being is summarized in another remarkable sentence. Unique object of his grandmother's care (with "her servant's livery, her nurse's uniform")—indeed, the object of a cult ("her religious habit")—this ridiculous god realizes that he exists only through his faithful: "I knew, when I was with my grandmother . . . that *everything that was mine*, my cares, my wishes, would be, in my grandmother, supported upon a desire to save and prolong my life stronger than was my own" (i, 507). *He is only the Other's desire*. Without the "support" (admire the clinical precision of the term) of the vital functions of another for his own needs, he does not even have a will to live. Better yet, "my thoughts were continued in her without having to undergo any deflection, since they passed from my mind into hers without change of atmosphere or of personality" (i, 507). Not only does the Narrator not have his own body, but he does not even have a psychic "atmosphere," his own "personality." His strange *cogito* is "My grandmother thinks, therefore I am." *He is, then, only what she thinks.*

It is not a question here of symbiosis but, strictly speaking, of parasitism. Such is clearly the biological model, the final nourishment that Proustian fantasy gives itself. In order to overcome the anguish of strong and weak beats, the alternation of fullness and emptiness, it goes down again from the infant to the fetus. At the end of the Balbec I scene, the Narrator calms his fright of desertion in the "unfamiliar" room ("I was utterly alone: I longed to die"; i, 507) by magically transforming this room into a protective uterus: "My bed is just on the other side, and the partition is quite thin" (i, 507). (The fantasy structure is faithfully reproduced with Albertine, as it should be: "The partition that divided our two dressing rooms . . . was so slender"; ii, 385).[6] It is a refuge where it suffices to give "three knocks" (i, 507) to have someone immediately willing "to give milk" to him. Here, protection is one with continuous nourishment. This is, of course, to overlook the fact that for the fetus, the "partition" is also a prison. In the grandmother's case, as in Albertine's, the desire for in-dependence will not cease until he has broken its walls. There is *always too much* love for this desire, because where love is concerned, the Other is *always de trop*. By a rigorous law, if the Other's continual presence determines absence to yourself, presence to yourself demands the Other's eternal absence—without whom it is, however, impossible to be yourself.

This formulation of the central crux of the neurosis enables us, on returning to the madeleine scene, to see how the ambivalence conflict functions here. The madeleine, we were saying, *is eaten*. Eating is euphoric repletion only from one perspective; from a completely different one, it is an essentially *destructive* act. There is no need to bring up "cannibalism," the oral sadistic impulse, or other fragments of ready-made theory; we have only to read the text: "After the things are broken and scattered, still, alone, more fragile, but with more vitality . . . more persistent, more faithful, the smell and taste of things remain poised a long time" (1, 36). There is no better way of saying that in order for *taste* to exist, there must be *destruction*.[7] Eating is a variety of murder. Françoise killing the chicken while crying "filthy creature," or torturing the kitchen maid with the cleaning of asparagus: these celebrated scenes suffice to recall the other side—not the pleasant but the cruel side of "Proustian foods."

Here, the incorporation of the madeleine (mother) is a highly aggressive act. As we have seen, the Narrator gobbles it up in one bite. From then on, it is a question only of mouthfuls of tea. In fact, madeleine and tea, the "good" and the "bad" food, are only metaphoric projections of a fundamental ambivalence toward the Mother—the location of a permanent affective reversal from "for" to "against." Because if we could previously assign the principal role in the experience to the negative tea, the contrary is also true: the tea's insistence is the madeleine's alibi. By denouncing the sinner (Madeleine) mother as a "poisoner," the Narrator projects *his own aggressivity* onto her; he devours her in order to appropriate her substance. By accusing the Other, he disguises his oral, then his anal sadism. The madeleine scene tells us, in fact, the story of a *digestion*. In order to find my identity: (1) I eat Mamma; (2) I digest Mamma; (3) I make Combray, "the whole of Combray and of its surroundings, taking their proper *shapes and growing solid*" (1, 36). If we recall that the pastry is "moulded in the fluted scallop," the anal fantasy is obvious. Except for one detail: everything taking shape and growing solid "sprang into being . . . from my cup of tea" (1, 36). The tea (liquid) cannot supply the substance for an excretion (solid). What is well "moulded" is the madeleine. The destructive assimilation, ingestion of the mother, is repressed in favor of the "tea," which moves deceptively on to what is essential. At this primitive level, "I make Combray" means "I shit Mamma." In fact, successful defecation presents the archaic model of an ideal constitution of the "self": (1) conversion of the Other into my own substance; (2) expulsion of the "bad" food, after absorption of the "good." If the madeleine experience is the story of a nutritive ecstasy, its ultimate place is the *toilet*.

This is doubly verified. One of the most important "reminiscence" scenes of the book, generally neglected in favor of the "madeleine" or of the "court flagstones," which "go down" better with Proust scholars, if I may say so, is that of the Champs-Elysées lavatory (1, 376–77), where "a chill and fusty smell" suddenly proposes to the Narrator "to descend into the underlying reality which it had not yet disclosed to me." In the "tenant of the establishment, an elderly dame with painted cheeks and an auburn wig," we recognize the mother by her *cheek*. Furthermore, this old woman calls herself "marquise": we are familiar enough with the value of the symbols "king" and "queen" in the interpretation of dreams. Besides, "Mamma" herself emerges twice in a few lines, as an instance of an *alimentary* taboo ("sweets . . . which, alas, Mamma would never allow me to take").

Without claiming to elucidate in detail a complex scene, I would like to consider, for the purpose of this discussion, the fact that the marquise/mother opens for the young boy "the hypogean doors of those cubicles of stone in which men crouch like sphinxes." Of course, whoever says "sphinx" says "Oedipus" but clearly, in this case, also says "sphincter." At this level, the riddle of identity passes through the stage of defecation mastery, more than through that of incest temptation: "In any event, if the 'marquise' had a weakness for little boys . . . she must have been moved to that generosity less by the hope of corrupting them than by the pleasure which all of us feel in displaying a needless prodigality to those whom we love" (I, 367–77).

Lavish (for her own pleasure) or repressive (no candy), sovereign dispenser of the alimentary *not enough* and *too much*, imposing the tormenting rhythm of *Fort-Da* in the domain of food as in that of sleep (the "hypogeum" joining the thematic series of "holes" of Combray I: "hollow of the bed," "monstrous funnel," etc.), the mother claims to control evacuation for the same reason that she controls the filling-up. In this astonishing scene, although he does not *need* it, "this 'marquise' . . . even opened one of her doors for me, saying: 'Won't you go inside for a minute? Look, here's a nice, clean one.'" Drama of "cleanliness": you must "make" on command. The infantile *do what you like* answers the maternal *do what you must*. Sphinx-sphincter: being *yourself* begins there. The toilet is the battlefield, the battle being a struggle for identity. If I cannot control the "entry" (madeleine, tea), I am master of the "exit" ("the whole of Combray . . . sprang into being").[8] If, at the beginning of the madeleine scene, the Narrator refuses the tea and then "changes his mind," in the lavatory scene he refuses "to make." In place of this, he will make Combray.

Even more than the Combray bedroom where the battle of the "kiss" takes place, less noble but perhaps even more intimate, the privileged place for the combat against the mother's ascendancy is the *toilet*. It is time to verify our initial hypothesis that there is a rigorous superimposition between masturbation scene and recollection act. If there is a homology of structure for such different manifest content, the two experiences, so dissimilar, must of course have an *identical meaning*. In order to be accurate, our intrepretation of the "madeleine" must be able, in some way, to fall back upon that of "masturbation," fold back in order that the texts coincide. In my opinion, this is clearly the case. "It was an unusually spacious room for a *water-closet*" (CSB, 30). The first text presents, so to speak, ingenuously, what the secondary elaboration hides: the "bedroom" where the Narrator remembers is the "toilet" where he masturbates. He remembers—but not the toilet (the street lavatory of the *Recherche* constituting a kind of "return of the repressed"). This is easily understandable. If the *memory of places,* as we have seen, establishes and supports the self's identity, the repression of the ambivalence conflict suppresses first the *place* of the violation, the better to hide its nature from this same self. The ecstasy of ejaculation clearly grants the ipseity that has been mystically sought: "At last a shimmering jet arched forth, spurt after spurt, as when the fountain at Saint-Cloud begins to play—which we can recognize (since there is *a personality* in the untiring flow of its waters"; (CSB, 31). But to see in it only a purely *positive* event is in fact to fail to recognize (and not to "recognize," as the passage invites us to do) the true function of the narcissistic orgasm. Enjoyment (of self) is possible only through *negation* (of the mother):

Far as the forest might stretch and the clouds round themselves *[in the shape of* "madeleines"*]* above it, I felt that my spirit extended a little farther, was not quite filled by it *[the extreme metaphorical persistence of the unconscious is astonishing here].* . . . I felt the lovely swelling hillsides *[madeleine-mother] that rose* like breasts *["cheeks" that are sucked] on either side of the river supported, like mere* insubstantial reflections, *on the dominating stare of my pupils.* All this world reposed on me, and I was more than it. [CSB, 30]

The "self" affirms itself through the rejection of the female imago. Ejaculation and defecation are two forms of maternal expulsion. More exactly, it's the formula of "reverse repletion": whereas "eating Mamma" *empties the self by filling it,* "shitting Mamma" and "pissing Mama" *fill the self by emptying it.* Without previous "emptying" of the Other, there is no advent of the self at all. For this reason, the "toilet" is the chosen place for the symbolic liberation. It's a question of knowing precisely by whom it is "occupied." "I paused to draw breath. Wishing to sit down without being incommoded by the sun which was shining full on the seat, I quoted to it: 'Take yourself off, my boy, to make room for me'" (CSB, 31).[9] This injunction gives us, undisguised, a "key" to the story. This maternal Word, this saying that indicates an intolerable intrusion, is turned against the occupying Power. In the struggle to death for identity, the Narrator bluntly declares: "It's me or it's her."

From then on, "to eat Mamma" (madeleine) and "to ejaculate Mamma" (masturbation) have the same meaning: *to kill Mamma*. It is through this ultimate meaning that the two disparate scenes become juxtaposed. At the bottom of the ambivalence conflict, the classic "death wish" is hidden. Manifest in Albertine's case ("'Just think, Albertine, if you were to meet with an accident!' Of course I did not wish her any harm. But what a pleasure it would be if, with her horses, she should take it into her head to ride off somewhere"; II, 463), it is displaced, spontaneously and openly, to the grandmother: "It seemed to me that, by my entirely selfish affection, I had allowed Albertine to die just as I had murdered my grandmother" (II, 734). Censorship blocks the deadly wish at the mother: here we undoubtedly have one of the reasons why Proust split the maternal figure into two instances, mother/grandmother, in the *Recherche:* one inviolable (she disappears ironically, without dying, by going *to take tea* at Mrs. Sazerat's; II, 985); the other made to suffer a violent death, tormented by a long illness.

In the *Contre Sainte-Beuve,* however, censorship is not effective; it permits the deadly image to break forth: in the pleasure of orgasm "a bitter smell, like the smell of sap, was mixed with it, as though I had snapped the branch" (CSB, 31). The wrong is quickly righted, and by the end of the scene the mother rises up again in the form of the lilacs, which are swaying "like elderly ladies who still preserve the mannered graces of their youth" (p. 32).

Repression is deeper in the *Recherche.* It would be almost perfect and the madeleine scene would be an edifying production if the good mother warming her chilly son did not receive, toward the end of the passage, a strange compensation in the line "when from a long-distant past nothing subsists, *after the people are dead*" (I, 36). In order that the "taste remain" (that the madeleine experience be possible), it is necessary that there be *"destruction des choses"* (that the madeleine be eaten): that is, that *the mother, whom we see offering tea, be dead.*

We are undoubtedly now in a position to answer our initial

question and to say precisely *what*, in the madeleine reminiscence, and short of the masturbatory experience, the screen-memory *screens*.

◀ 6 ▶

Yet things would be too simple if the mother's "death" or "murder" were the son's liberation. Certainly, the aggressive thrust—visible in certain episodes (confrontation in Venice); transparent in others (Golo nursing evil intentions against Geneviève de Brabant, quite rightly the story of a "projection"); elsewhere carefully repressed (madeleine)—this "hostility for the mother" is very strong throughout. But lo and behold, it is proportional to the need. *With* this "alter ego" you could not be yourself; neither can you live *without* it. We cannot omit one of the terms of the problem. This invading Other, who must be *suppressed*, is impossible *to do without*. In the *Contre Sainte-Beuve* text, as we've seen, no sooner has the son "killed" the mother than he revives her. In the *Recherche* it is even better: he eliminates one half (grandmother) in order to keep the second (mother), which he completes by also retaining Françoise— so true is it that, for the Narrator, you are never so well "served" as by others. Not for an instant has he conquered his "independence." On the very threshold of the *Temps retrouvé*, he has not "grown up" at all. When he asks Gilberte de Saint-Loup to come to dine with him if she doesn't find it compromising to "be seen dining alone with a young man" (ii, 1039), and when everyone laughs at his slip, he observes: "I realised that the remark that had made them laugh was one that my mother, to whom I was always a child, might have made in speaking of me." From the beginning to the end of the *Recherche*, from the Combray i "kiss" to the "Guermantes reception," nothing in this respect has changed, and nothing is served in the end when the mother disappears, if, for her as much as for yourself, you continue to remain *a child*.

The very terms of the neurosis offer its solution. Strength is knowing how to use your weakness. The *real* failure will become *imaginary* success. If (as has been repeated time and again) the ultimate goal of the *Recherche* is to show, through the faults of a man, the "birth of a writer," the aim of this analysis is the same; to employ the "psychocritical" instrument is in no way to use literary texts in order to illustrate a psychiatric picture (if such were our claim, it would be quite useless; concerning Proust, we would be, from a clinical point of view, only beating a horse that has been dead a long time). It's a matter, on the contrary, thanks to a "psychoreading" of the texts, of understanding them differently and, in my opinion, better; it's a matter of grasping, in the *partial* data of what they "say," the very thing that is "not said" and that they "want to say." It is a question of having them say not *anything other* than what they say but *all* they say—or, more modestly, to try to do so.

Of course, an exhaustive "local" elucidation, at the very level at which we are situated—and many others exist—is not possible. In order "to exhaust" the meaning of the "madeleine," literally the whole book would be necessary. It cannot be fully understood *on the spot*. Once again, the Narrator is right in presenting this experience both as a matrix and as something unexplained. Whether you adopt his interpretive system or ours, there is no possible comprehension until the end of the *Temps retrouvé*. The scene clearly functions as a cipher for the entire *Recherche*, which—given that its last lines echo the first—turns out to be, to the end, the quest for a kind of ipseity: "All this long stretch of time . . . had been uninterruptedly lived, thought, secreted by me . . . it was . . . my very self" (II, 1123). To try to restore the passage's multiple levels of meaning, then, it is necessary for criticism to extend its network to the rest of the work. The elucidation of the madeleine, representative of the Proustian construct, is transformed into an introduction to a psychoreading of the *Recherche*. Such a reading is not "objective" or "innocent"; wedding the desire of the text, it inserts itself at the very location of its inquiry. To "fill" the intervals, the gaps, is to fully satisfy its wishes: to speak the *madeleine's language*—to "mould" critical discourse in its "fluted shell." The interpreter, first a "son" of the text and turned against it, becomes its "mother." He feeds it with his substance. The writer has the critic play all his roles, as he did Albertine. Like it or not, commentary enters into the nutritive circuit of the work. The deciphering grid will then supply the text with current, unmasking in its operation the disguised *function*. Like the analyst for the patient, analytic criticism will be for the text the support and pivot of its fantasies.

Nearly at the end of the *Temps retrouvé*, we find the Narrator grown old without having ever been adult. He remains a child to the end, at the price of the suffering that he both endures and inflicts, as we have seen. Seeking his independent being, he exists only as a parasite. Then, in the courtyard of the Guermantes residence, the unevenness of the paving blocks reveals pure Time to him; he experiences ecstasy; saved, he will become the writer.

Let us in turn see what happens. What occurs in the final illumination? "Our true self, which had long seemed dead but was not dead in other ways, awakes, takes on fresh life as it receives the *celestial nourishment* brought to it" (II, 996). He who has tasted "a fragment of time in its pure state" finds his "nourishment" only in "the essence of things." An extraordinary rigor, I would even say rigidity, supports the whole *Recherche*: the entire space it covers is that which, immense and infinitesimal, separates "celestial" nourishment from earthly, imaginary from real, *that which you fill with your self* and *that which fills the self*. In both cases, the model is identical. It remains that of maternal nutrition, but reversed, as Marx has "put back on its feet" Hegel's dialectic. The original nourishment is the first alienation. All alone, the Narrator cannot sleep (he sends for his mother for the "kiss"); he is unable to eat (his mother sends for the madeleine); he is incapable of looking after himself ("seeing that I was cold"). All alone, he has no being. Everything *is given* by another. Even the "celestial nourishment," in the final illumination of pure Time, is "brought to him." The quest for self is your downfall. You have no being *of your own* other than the one you *give* yourself. Everything happens as if the long march of the Proustian unconscious were leading to the formula: *to be yourself, you will become your own mother.* What is not possible in the real is executed in the imaginary, through art. The "singularity," the "individuality," whose search he has undertaken, is *inaccessible in existence.* Someone is no one. The self—is other people. Who better than the Narrator has described and understood, from snobbism to love, from patriotism to politics, the subtle network of an infinite alienation? But while he is listening to the septet, "the phrases of Vinteuil" give an impression "different from any other, as though, notwithstanding the conclusions to which science seems to point, the individual did really exist" (II, 558). We must go still further. The "individual" is found nowhere else, it is nothing else. "That ineffable something which makes a difference of quality between what each of us has felt and what he is obliged to leave behind at the threshold of . . . phrases . . . art, the art of a Vinteuil like that of an Elstir, makes . . . apparent, rendering externally visible . . . that intimate composition of those worlds which we call individual persons, and which, without the aid of art, we should never know" (II, 559). Clearly, we arrive here at what is essential in the Narrator's discovery. You *are* never yourself, unless you *create yourself* in a language.

Thus, still more than "self-contemplation" (II, 490), the work of art is an autogenesis. You *give birth to yourself*. The maternity relationship is in no way denied but assumed and reversed. The ultimate discovery refers back to the original model. The "end" is none other than the "beginning"—reversed. In this way, at the level of fantasy, the celebrated "circularity" of the Proustian corpus takes shape. From childhood, we could say that the writer has neither forgotten nor learned anything. In a way, he only revolves around the same mode of existence, reverses it. At no time can he get out of it. Aseity and ipseity, the objects of the quest, constitute an imaginary mothering, where, as with Albertine, but this time without role confusion or permutation, he *himself* will be *the mother*, and *the work* will be *the child*—"literature taking up again the abandoned labors of the amorous illusion" (II, 1020). Upon conception (if I may say so), the book gives the Narrator, as Leo Bersani has noticed, the physical symptoms of pregnancy. Once it is born, how do you nourish it? You must "*le suralimenter comme un enfant*" (Pléiade III, 1032): not feed, but "overfeed it like a child." Between his work and himself, the writer can only (knows only how to) reenact the type of relationship that existed between himself and his mother—and not only from the point of view of nourishment: in the *Temps retrouvé* the celebrated series of metaphors concerning the Book to come testifies that

this writer . . . would need to prepare it with minute care, constantly regrouping his forces as if for an attack, endure it like an exhausting task, accept it like a rule of conduct, build it like a church, follow it like a regimen, overcome it like an obstacle, win it like a friendship . . . create it like a world. [ii, 1112]

To all appearances incoherent, or simply cumulative, the series of comparisons is governed and generated, at bottom, by the *maternal metaphor* from which it derives its rigorous unity. The disjointed terms of the enumeration, as a matter of fact, systematically explore mother-child relations as the Narrator has experienced them in their fundamental ambivalence. These relations constitute interaction, or rather, as the text says, "regrouping of forces." As an object embodying a permanent "attack" and "exhausting task," an eternal "obstacle" for the mother, the child is nevertheless a "rule of conduct," a "regimen" of life. His education ("building") is a sacred duty ("church"), a thankless task of "creation" from which, as a reward for this patient modeling, she hopes to obtain a "friendship."

Metaphoric combination, as in the case of the madeleine scene, is strengthened by metonymic selection at the narrative level. Confined in the Guermantes' library, which serves as a waiting room, the Narrator conceives his book surrounded by books. A fine scholar, in order to justify his plan, he appeals to the example of illustrious predecessors: Chateaubriand, Nerval, Baudelaire. Yet the only *real* book that a sudden impulse makes him snatch from the shelves is in no way one of the "great books." It is the modest *François le Champi*, bearing Combraysian memories: "That stranger was . . . the child I had been in those days, aroused within me by this book. . . . this book, which my mother had read aloud to me at Combray almost until early morning" and which had "retained for me all the spell of that night" (ii, 1005). Just as, from the point of view of the work's conception, the writer repeats the feeding ritual (madeleine), from the point of view of its execution, he re-enacts his nighttime rituals (bedtime drama). The last pages of the *Recherche* "fall back" with astonishing precision upon the first. They set up the exact—I was going to say, the rigid—correspondence between writing and neurosis: "Only in the daytime, at best, might I try to sleep. If I worked, it would be only at night" (II, 1120). A rigorous, unconscious equation at this point establishes a substitution relation among the narrator's activities, which are to all appearances unrelated. The system of "giving birth through art" remains locked in the childhood structure—waking/sleeping (depersonalization/identity). Liberation consists in placing the act of writing at the very location of slavery: the enjoyment of the "self" is finally—with time—recaptured at the usual scene of its loss.

Yet if Marcel, from among all the Guermantes' books, takes from the shelf *François le Champi*, this gesture has a meaning even more precise. With a knowledge, quasi-infallible in Proust, of the topography of the unconscious, he refers to a specific "trace": "To read the subjective book of these strange signs . . . no one could help me with any rule, for the *reading* of that book is a creative act in which no one can stand in our stead, or even collaborate with us. And therefore how many there are who shrink from *writing* it" (II, 1001). If this Proustian theory of writing *as* reading seems at first glance enigmatic, it takes on particular meaning if we think of the Combray I bedtime scene, incurable wound from which, in the end, emerges the Book.

This scene, served as an hors-d'oeuvre or "*hors-texte*," bears the mark of the writer's "vocation" well before it is affirmed or conscious. It determines, for the Proustian Narrator, the very meaning of his future activity. At the level of fantasy, where real conflicts project imaginary solutions, writing is the *only outcome* possible for the "undressing drama" (I, 33). If "the strongest desire I had in the world, namely, to keep my mother in my room through the sad hours of darkness," clashes with a fundamental taboo ("ran too much counter to general requirements and to the wishes of others"; I, 33), it is obvious that in the Oedipal structure the satisfaction of "reading," which is granted, functions for the child as a substitute for sexual gratification, which is refused—and which he will refuse himself later in his adult life, always valuing imaginary satisfaction in sexual relations.

It is understood that in another "psychocritical" sorting board the system of *paternal identifications* (the father, Swann, Bergotte, Charlus) or *fraternal* ones (Bloch, Saint-Loup) should be carefully analyzed—but this is not the place. In the limited framework of this study, I will restrict myself to a single level of the text: that of the dual relations with the mother, as we have defined them. "Reading" will enter the "parasitic" system with which we are becoming familiar; in this scene, contiguous to that of the madeleine, the mother stuffs him with words, as she will fill him with cake— with, furthermore, in this parallel repletion, the same curious "gap": "When it was Mamma who was reading to me aloud she left all the love-scenes out" (1, 32). In both cases, at both levels (existential, symbolic), the mother (re)produces; the son consumes. In the absence of liberation, which is impossible in the domain of the real and forbidden in the domain of the imaginary (with Gilberte and Albertine, he weaves again the very web in which he was previously caught), *to create yourself is to (re)produce yourself in the symbolic register*, through an imaginary maternity that is a real neurosis.

Such, it seems, is the central equation that generates Proustian writing. In the tension-filled competition for being, which becomes a struggle for language supremacy, the Narrator will finally take his place (hers, the mother's) by repossessing this "mother tongue." By way of an initial equation, (1) *writing = reading in the mother's place*. The edifying and moving narrative of the nighttime reading at Combray allows the hostile impulse to break through. At the very time that the "hero"—to use this classical Proustian nomenclature—lulls himself to "George Sand's prose," the "Narrator," on the contrary, denounces that "moral distinction which Mamma had *learned from my grandmother* to place above all other qualities in life, and which *I was not to teach her* until much later to refrain from placing, in the same way, above all other qualities in literature" (1, 32).

The essential opposition life/books, in which, for Proust, the book is the "true life," is in this way linked to a reversal of roles: subject to the mother in "life," in the domain of "books" he becomes, as is so rightly said, "her master." The unconscious adds, *her mother*, since to become the mother's educator is to take the "grandmother's place." Thus, to become "the mother's mother"— fantasy of imaginary maternity that he constantly acts out, and in vain with Albertine—is the only way *to give birth to yourself*, provided that you *situate being in language*. Since there is (and the child lost in his imaginary Combray "readings" and "voyages" knew it well before the Narrator's pseudodiscovery) no possible place to assure ipseity other than the milieu of language, whether it be words, sounds, or colors—Bergotte's, Vinteuil's, or Elstir's—to be your own mother or to become your mother's mother *is to be able to read to yourself*. To be yourself is *to find your own voice, to find yourself*. This "act of creation," which the *Temps retrouvé* defines, "in which no one can stand in our stead, or even collaborate with us," in which "no one could help me with any rule," is none other than an emblem in which the "reading scene" is itself legible. Identity is the *authentic*—that is, the *singular*—production of a language.

Enchanting, lulling, satisfying, or soporific, the maternal voice remains an *alienated* one. She reads aloud "phrases which *seemed* to have been composed for her voice. . . . She came to them with the tone they required, with the cordial accent which *existed before* they were, which *dictated* them" (I, 33). Pretense of identity, it's a *trompe-l'oreille* (fooling of the ear), since the maternal voice only recaptures someone else's "accent," places itself *at the service of the Other*. (The relationship between the Berma and *Phèdre* should certainly be studied in this connection.) A "dictated" tone is always a dictatorship. In the creator that Vinteuil embodies, the reverse occurs: "Whatever be the question asked, it is in *the same accent*, that is to say *its own*, that it replies" (II, 558). Achieving "his own essential nature" is nothing other than finding this "unique accent," which is the only "*véritable différence*" (Pléiade III, 256).

We now understand why Proust displays a mania for "conversation," which he samples in the course of unending dialogues. What the Narrator's implacable ear hears in all *collective* languages (Verdurin salons, Grand Hotel coteries, Guermantes clans, etc.) and in all *individual* codes (Odette's anglicisms, Saint-Loup's speeches, Albertine's slang, the Balbec manager's blunders) is *clichés*. In all possible forms, including "noble" ones (intellectual, political, or patriotic), he pursues them. His obsession is *tracking them down*. If the Narrator "speaks" so little himself, whether in reticence or ruse, he knows that he does not escape the law. In his valuable study "Proust et le language indirect," Gérard Genette remarks, "Language is, in the world of the *Recherche*, one of the great revealers of snobbism."[10] It is a question of one and the same *alienation*, whether social or verbal: if you desire what others desire, you speak the speech of someone else. To break the circle of alienations, to coincide with yourself, to find your "accent," like Vinteuil, to achieve "your own essence" is nothing more—and nothing less— than that, to suspend "preexisting dictation." To be yourself is *to invent your own language*.

Until now we have not taken into account the "invention" itself of Proust's language as such. Our only intention is to show *to what function* the *functioning* of writing corresponds in Proust. Is it possible to "go back," however, from the psychic structures that condition the writing enterprise to the writing procedures that produce this enterprise? Or again, if we consider the particular relation of a writer to language (which every literary text necessarily reflects) as constituting the "deep structure" of the articulation process, is it possible to generate, by a system of transformations, the way in which this deep structure projects itself upon the "surface structure" of the terminal text? Were such a "generative" criticism nonexistent, we would have the right to dream of it and certainly to attempt the experiment, even if we should finally decide that it is impossible. Until now, the psychocritical approach has remained essentially static and structural. It seems to study works in repose. The dynamism it introduces is an imported one, having recourse to biography. It is, of course, legitimate to listen, through the text, to the history of a person—and the criticism inspired by analysis,

with Freud at its head, does not deprive itself of this. But the opposite seems more interesting to me, in any case more in accord
with the literary critic's intention: through the history of a person,
to listen to the *history of a text*. To eavesdrop in the text upon the
narration of its genesis, where could we better attempt the experiment than in this *Recherche*, where a man relates the birth of his
vocation as a writer? We must execute the analytic operation, as
far as that is possible, in the opposite direction. We must try to go
not from discourse to the production of symptoms, but *from symptoms to the production of discourse*. Such is, at least, the direction
in which we would like to have this inquiry progress at this point
in our own discourse.

◀ 7 ▶

To be yourself, to invent your own language. We will try to follow
the carrying out of this Proustian imperative, to take hold of it in
the different stages in which the *desire for language* is formed and
transformed. We probably understand better why the Narrator says
that "nature" put him on "the true path of art" and how she is "herself a beginning of art" (II, 1009).

Proustian writing takes shape (once again) during the scene of
the nighttime reading of *François le Champi*, "contemplated for the
first time in my little room at Combray during what was, perhaps,
the sweetest and saddest night of my life . . . and rediscovered today
in the Guermantes library on the most beautiful day of my life, as
it happened, when a great light suddenly shone, not only on the
old gropings of my thought, but even on the purpose of my life and,
perhaps, of art itself" (II, 1006–7). The reversal by which the "saddest night" becomes "the most beautiful day," is, to use the text's
categories, the changing of "lived" life into "written" life. But what
exactly is the meaning of the well-known Proustian theme: "True
life, life disclosed at last and made clear . . . is literature"? What
is this "disclosure" that makes life clear, that transforms "life"
into "art"?

We again come upon all the recipes of Proustian cooking in
a literary confection: "Would I not be making my book the way

Françoise made her *boeuf à la mode* so liked by M. de Norpois, the jelly of which was enriched by so many carefully selected pieces of meat?" (II, 1114). The nutritive obsession lives in the fantasies of writing. Style, for example in Flaubert, becomes a device or, rather, a process by which "all the elements of reality are rendered down into one unanimous substance. . . . No flaw remains in it. . . . Everything at variance with it has been *made over* and *absorbed*. In Balzac, on the other hand, all the elements of a style which is still to come exist together, undigested and untransformed" (CSB, 170). Conversion, absorption, nutrition: written life, the "true" life, is *a digested life*. A parallel concoction transforms ("makes over") madeleine into nourishing substance, and words into stylistic substance. But although real nourishment comes from the Other, attesting a fundamental alienation, the "one substance" in which no "flaw" (*impureté*, in the French) has remained, in which "everything at variance" is "absorbed," this verbal substance in the pure state is "me." With words, *I have digested the Other*. The digested Other is the mother. In this way, the two contiguous and superficially opposed scenes, that of the kiss and that of the madeleine, are phantasmally fused.

The Narrator says without hesitation, regarding Albertine: "Unfortunately, since love tends to the *complete assimilation of another person*, while other people are not *comestible by way of conversation alone*, Albertine might be (and indeed was) as friendly as possible to me on our way home . . . she left me happy but more famished for her even than I had been at the start" (I, 693–94). After the nighttime reading, and although she has been "as kind as possible," Mamma will leave the child, in this voyage to the end of the night, "more famished for her." The reason is precise: someone else is not "comestible by way of conversation alone," since, when you speak, your words are "in the mouth of the Other." If we have been able to say, in a previous equation, that (1) "to write = to read in the mother's place" (to give yourself the nourishment of the kiss through an ideal maternity that suppresses the need for the real mother), at a still more archaic level, (2) "to write = to eat the words of the Other"—as we say "eat your words"—so that the

Other becomes "indistinct" in language; that is, its existence as Other is suppressed in language. The "suppression of someone else," necessary for "the complete assimilation of another person," is not possible as long as there is "conversation." In the form of the voice, dialogue posits the Other as presence. Writing's silence will finally be its absence. "To write," as to eat, is "to kill."

Here again, the *boeuf mode* aspect of the book, like the "confection" aspect of the madeleine, is only the pleasant side, the smiling face of the nutritive process. There is also the opposite side of the coin. The functioning of writing has the same meaning as the digestive function: "The work of art is a work of death." It remains completely locked in the neurotic structure of a "death wish" for the one you love best. In the case of Proust, and as the analysis of the madeleine shows, the complete unconscious formula would be "to write or to eat is *to kill the mother*." If it is necessary to confirm this analysis, we have only to refer once again to the masturbation scene in the *Contre Sainte-Beuve*, which underlies the madeleine scene. At the moment when the Narrator brings himself to orgasm—a solitary pleasure, that is, the conquest of his own being ("personality" of the "shimmering jet")—through the imaginary suppression of his mother ("Take yourself off, my boy"), what occurs when he has "snapped the branch"? "I had left a *trail* on the *leaf*, silvery and natural as a thread of gossamer or a snail-track, that was all. But on that bough, it seemed to me like the *forbidden fruit on the Tree of Knowledge* and like the races that give non-human forms to their deities for some time afterward it was in the guise of *this almost interminably extensible silvery thread which I had to spin out of myself* by going widdershins to the normal course of my life that I pictured *the devil*" (CSB, 31).

"Trail" left upon a "leaf," "thread" (*fil*) which you can extend "almost interminably" and which you can "spin out of" yourself: by a remarkable ambiguity, the description of the masturbation act is, word for word, appropriate to the writing act. Anticipating the *Recherche*, this description defines the very project of writing with astonishing precision: in its *end* (to create its own substance), in its *means* (the "thread" of written matter almost indefinitely stretched out), even in its *narrative technique* (the originally "natural trail" is inscribed "by going widdershins to the normal course of my life": deconstruction, circularity of the narrative that reverses itself). This metaphoric prescience, which unknowingly identifies the "jet of sperm" and the "springing forth of writing," guesses their common desire: "to make yourself the source of your being" by suppressing "the maternal source of being." Such a reversal of the normal "course of events" is experienced as "antiphysis," an enterprise at once "sacred" ("deities") [11] and "maleficent" ("forbidden fruit on the Tree of Knowledge," "devil"). Writing as a sublimated act of masturbation immediately assigns its lethal statute to the literary work.

We know the famous quotation: "A book is a great cemetery in which one can no longer decipher the half-effaced names on most of the graves" (II, 1018–19). An initial reason for this is given in another not less well-known statement: "All these materials for literary work were . . . my past life" (II, 1015–16). A "past life," especially if it is already long, is necessarily a "cemetery" where we find many dead. The analytic interpretation adds: "The dead whom you *find* are above all those whom you have *put* there. The "names" are not, moreover, so "effaced" on Proustian tombs that we cannot clearly read those of Albertine, whom Marcel has "allowed to die" (II, 1018), or of his grandmother, whom he "murdered" (II, 734). When the Narrator says: "All these beings, who had revealed truths to me and who were no longer living, seemed to me to have lived lives *that had benefitted no one but me*, and to have died *for me*" (II, 1018), the analyst translates: they are dead *through* me and *for* my own profit. But how? While the Narrator proposes that those he loved "were in the last analysis merely posing for him, as it is with painters" (II, 1020), the study of the madeleine substitutes a different version for this sweetened and "academic" one: he took advantage of those he loved in the sense in which we say that a child "is thriving"—by *feeding* upon them. In a much less innocent way, he has not simply "used" them once they are dead; he has *devoured them alive*. The "materials" of the literary work are first a living "material" that has been parasitically absorbed. If "nature," to take up once again his formula, has placed the Narrator "on the true path of art," the vampirism of his book only takes to its extreme the vampirism of his life.

We must rid the cruel Proustian work of the aestheticizing pieties with which we—and often Proust himself—have covered it over. We should—otherwise this analysis of the madeleine would be useless—return it to its evil ways. Bataille perfectly well, and for good reason, felt this: Proust is the "artist of evil" he tells us about. But what Bataille showed above all for the erotic scenes should be extended to the entire writing process: for Proust, literature *is* evil. If not, we would not understand the paradox that he underlines in the supreme lucidity of the *Temps retrouvé*. While "writing comprise[s] for the writer a healthful and indispensable function, the fulfilling of which brings happiness, as do[es] for a man of a physical type exercise" (II, 1018), its practice is accompanied by a feeling of *inextinguishable guilt*. It is also interesting to notice that the euphoric surface, visible only in *physical* activities (masturbation, madeleine), becomes torn by the torturing ambivalence that can no longer be repressed. You write to punish yourself. You punish yourself to expiate your crimes: "Oh, might I *in expiation*, when my work should be completed, wounded beyond relief and abandoned by all, suffer for long and weary hours before I died!" (II, 1018)—a cry from the innermost self that condemns the writer to his torture.

We must take the "agony" dear to postromanticism literally. One must suffer in order to write. This "will to suffer," a genuine need of the martyr, haunts the last pages of the work. It returns as an untiring litany: "Happiness is beneficial for the body, but it is grief that develops the powers of the mind. . . . As for happiness, it has hardly more than one useful quality, namely to make unhappiness possible. . . . Happy years are wasted years; we wait for suffering before setting to work" (II, 1020, 1021, 1023). To die, as the conclusion to his work, as the "final touch," is the death wish turned back upon the writer as punishment.

But since in order to write, one must of course remain alive, the Narrator gives himself a minimal existence: he lives, so to speak, "on the fringes of death." Total reclusion, night work, mimes a vital absence. A strange disease pushes him to the outermost boundary: "This obscure sense of what was going to happen was conveyed to me by the strange thing which occurred before I had begun my book. . . . three times I nearly fell as I went down the stairs. I was away only two hours and yet, when I got home, I felt as if I had no memory, no power to think, no strength, no life at all" (II, 1117). A "strange" attack, actually, occurring just in time to punish being "away," leaving him, as we so appropriately say, "all but dead." We can now understand the well-known sentence: "This idea of death settled permanently within me as does love for a woman" (II, 1119). To write is, literally speaking, to settle permanently in death.

We must, however, be careful not to understand this "settling" as the simple effect of masochism, itself a turning back of the sadistic impulse upon itself. These loose categories do not bring sufficient precision to bear upon Proust's enterprise. The supreme formulation is in the text: if death "settles" itself within you "as does love," it is because *it is a form of love*—to be exact, a refined manifestation of *necrophilia*. Writing is, in the strict sense, an act of *perversion*. Once again the erotic equation of the *Contre Sainte-Beuve* underlies the entire movement of Proustian writing. If the masturbation act transforms "the lovely swelling hillsides that rose like breasts" into "mere insubstantial reflections" through the window, incestuous desire takes on a particular aspect in Proust: "to have pleasure" (jet of sperm or of ink) "is to possess your dead mother." Here the Oedipal complex is resolved by way of a detour through the "tomb." We should recall the "hypogeum" at the Champs-Elysées (resting place, let us not forget, of the souls of the dead) where the "old marquise" tries to seduce the young boy in that location where men crouch "like sphinxes."

The fantasy will become explicit in what is well known as "Albertine's sleep": "I felt at such moments that I had been possessing her more completely, like an unconscious and unresisting object of dumb nature" (II, 428). This "object" will be identified further on by name: "'Come to my room in five minutes . . . afterwards I shall fall asleep at once, for I am almost dead.' It was indeed a dead woman that I beheld when, presently, I entered her room" (II, 632). If the neurotic (or ontological) demand is: "I want to be with-the-Other-without-the-Other-to-be-myself," its translation in sexual desire will be "I am myself" (the only one awake) "with the Other" (object submitted to my pleasure) "without the Other" (she had disappeared). To have pleasure/to write, is, then, ideally to masturbate upon a tomb. Let us recall once again what happens during "Albertine's sleep." Let us also think of Edgar Allan Poe: as solitary as it believes itself to be, perversion is never alone.

Of course, a lethiferous love of this kind is experienced as a "profanation." Through the window at Montjouvain (window again, as in the case of the masturbation that murders), Mlle Vinteuil's friend, as a prelude to pleasure, spits upon the portrait of the dead father (I, 125). In this way, too, writing takes up again, *consummates*, the sense (the essence) of the sexual act by offering, by prostituting Albertine to the readers of the book: "the *profanation* of one of my memories by unknown readers I had already consummated ahead of them. I was not far from feeling horror of myself" (II, 1018). But precisely, if in the case of Mlle Vinteuil and her friend "her adoration of her father was the primary condition of his daughter's sacrilege" (II, 562), the sacrilege in its turn *manifests* adoration—as is shown in the outcome of the story in which Mlle Vinteuil's friend, "by spending years in pouring over the cryptic scroll left by him," assures "the composer whose grey hairs she had sent in sorrow to the grave an immortal compensating glory" (II, 562).

If we go from sexuality to writing, from Mlle Vinteuil and Company to the Narrator, we understand better the meaning of the "expiation" that the artist's work constitutes. It is in no way a question of a sterile flagellation. To say expiation is to say not simple self-punishment but retrieval. To write—and it is certainly in this regard a privileged form of love—is to *save the one you love from oblivion*. At the level that interests us here, such is the underlying meaning of the "madeleine," the movement by which everything negative turns back into the positive: *the sacred function of mem-*

ory. To assure "an immortal and compensating glory" for the alter ego who is adored/profaned, loved/hated in the hell of ambivalence means literally *to compensate for* the real evil you have done—that is, for the unconscious, imaginary *death* you have desired—by conferring symbolic *immortality* (the language of music or of literature). With a new circle of the interpretive spiral, we must reverse the preceding proposition. If the artist, in effect, installs himself in death, he does so the better to fight it, to deny death by inventing an afterlife. The unconscious literally kills so that the written word may literally resuscitate.

We have already remarked in the *Contre Sainte-Beuve* text that the mother, suppressed in the masturbation orgasm, reappears in the form of the lilies that sway "like elderly ladies" (CSB, 32) at the end of the passage. In the conclusion of this diabolic experience, and as expiation, a genuine "resurrection" takes place before us— which, as Philippe Lejeune so clearly saw, constitutes one of the meanings of the "Madeleine complex" and of the entire *Recherche*. But if the "elderly ladies" are reborn at the level of fantasy, they reappear as well at the level of writing, in a *specifically Proustian* form: the shrubs were "swaying their plumed heads and supple frames like elderly ladies who still preserve the mannered graces of their youth, the lilac-scent came to meet us, welcoming us" (CSB, 31–32). That is to say, the mother's face is reborn in a figure of speech, in *metaphor*. Being familiar with Proust's obsession with this trope—his redefinitions, his constant mention of it, often without much rigor—we cannot help suspecting a genuine function of *fantasy* in the functioning of stylistics (which has been studied thoroughly in recent works).

Among the numerous formulations Proust gives along the way, the most celebrated, which culminates in the "theory of metaphor" of the *Temps retrouvé*, holds our attention. It speaks of "the only true relationship, which the writer must recapture so that he may forever link together in his phrase its two distinct elements. . . . comparing similar qualities in two sensations, he makes their essential nature stand out clearly by joining them in a metaphor, in order to remove them from the contingencies of time" (II, 1008–9).

In this sense, the madeleine experience, by "comparing similar qualities in two sensations," and by making "their essential nature" stand out, appears to be the existential foundation of a figure of speech. In other words, as we have already stated and will take up again in detail, the madeleine constitutes a "metaphor of metaphor," similar, moreover, to other Proustian experiences of the same type.

But what does that mean from the perspective of this analysis? For the combinatory logic of the unconscious that we are attempting to establish, "to remove them from the contingencies of time" (theory of metaphor), corresponds exactly to the symbolic series: "writing/masturbation/remembering = rendering immortal" (articulating desire). There is not simply an equivalence in the realm of the signified, but also the insistence of the signifier: referring to the texts previously quoted (madeleine, *Recherche*; masturbation, CSB), we find again, to the letter, the opposition "essence/contingency." *One* quality common to *two* sensations, miraculously reunited in *one* (common) essence: who will not recognize in this the neurotic equation $1 + 1 = 1$, the insatiable and impossible demand for symbiotic fusion, the obsession (which has been adequately described) with "unity and duality" that is at the center of the Narrator's deepest desire?

If we remain in any way doubtful, let's look even more closely at this curious "stylistic" definition: metaphor is this "only true relationship, which the writer must recapture so that he may forever link together in his phrase its two distinct elements." Clearly we are at the antipodes of the well-known meeting of the sewing machine and the umbrella on the operating table. Far from being a gratuitous invention in the realm of the imaginary, a *departure* into something unknown, Proustian metaphor is a *return* (which is why you must "recapture," not capture, a relation; which explains why the writer's task, according to the famous formula, is that of a "translator"). As "distinct" as the "elements" may be, the "only true relationship" must exhume the lost paradise that is organic unity. It is not a question here of the "mysterious and profound" Baudelairean unity or of a Swedenborgian nostalgia, but of an obsessional neurosis transposed to the level of language. The "only true relationship" between "two distinct elements" must be "forever linked together."

The incarceration fantasy reappears with all its force. You "imprison" the terms, as you "imprison" women, in order to assure a permanent nutritive circuit. Style is nothing but another Proustian prison: the writer takes two different objects, "establishes their relationship," and "encloses them in the necessary rings of a beautiful style" (II, 1008–9). Four walls are not enough: "He encloses them . . . in rings." With words, you can go further than with Albertine. "Nature" obviously puts you "on the true path of art," is a "beginning of art," but in art you can carry to its extreme the fantasy that is forbidden in life—unless, of course, you mimic this fantasy like Charlus. In his brothel, a *maison close* which he transforms into an imaginary jail, he is "chained to a bed like Prometheus to his rock" (II, 955); he is even "nicknamed, by allusion to a newspaper which was being published at that time, *l'Homme Enchaîné*" (II, 959). But while Charlus dreams of an infernal prison, the Narrator invents a "paradisiac prison" for himself.

What then are the "two objects" that are to be "enclosed" in the "rings" of style? Or again—to ask the same question—what are these two objects that are now one, provided they be removed from contingency (that is, from real life)? The dual relation between mother and son that structures the madeleine fantasy at every level projects in this way its ultimate avatar—the Narrator's poignant wish at the end of "The Heart's Intermissions": "I asked nothing better of God, if a Paradise exists, than to be able, there, to knock upon that wall the three little raps which my grandmother would know among a thousand . . . and that He would let me remain with her throughout eternity which would not be too long for us" (II, 118). *Us: me-with-her-forever.* The "wall" is resurrected only to attest to the fusion. *Standing out by reason of their common essence, joined one to the other, removed from the contingencies of time:* such is the metaphoric epiphany.

As the *Contre Sainte-Beuve* text indicated naively, so to speak, metaphor is, in writing, the place of the mother's resurrection—

more precisely still, the magic close in which mother and son "are transported," if it is true that (according to its etymology) metaphor constitutes the "transportation" of a meaning. You will say, we are very far from the madeleine. But no, we have never left it. If, in order to explore its semantic networks, we have had recourse to the rest of the work, just as a dream is analyzed by the systematic relation of elements that are discrete and often apparently distant, the place to which this study takes us back is always the place of the madeleine. Because, in the text, what do we find *in place of the madeleine*, I mean *once the madeleine is swallowed?* Combray in general? That's saying too much. Instantaneous memory makes two madeleines—past and present—coincide, makes an "Aunt Léonie-madeleine" emerge in place of the "Mamma-madeleine" ("the taste was that of the little crumb of madeleine which on Sunday mornings my Aunt Léonie used to give me"; 1, 36). The substitution of Aunt Léonie for Mamma is not the only textual transformation. The madeleine, offered by Mamma with "tea," is offered by the aunt after she dips it "first in her own cup of real or lime-flower tea" (1, 36). As early as the second paragraph of the same page, the "real" tea is elided; nothing remains but the "lime-flowers" ("the taste of the crumb of madeleine soaked in her decoction of lime-flowers which my aunt used to give me"). The substitution of Aunt Léonie for Mamma is that of lime-flowers for tea, of the tranquilizing drink for the insomnia-producing stimulant, of the *good* for the *bad* mother.

What is a "good mother"? The answer given by the unconscious is immediate: the one who gives the "good object." Here the "good object" is a double object, *lime-flowers-madeleine*, instead of the "bad object," *tea-madeleine*. If because of its "fluted shell" side the madeleine is clearly the female genitals (as Philippe Lejeune identifies it), because of the other side, which is "puffy," the cake obviously has the shape of the "breast." Genitals and breast—this is certainly the mother. It is also the madeleine, her ideal metaphor. Tea-Madeleine, the breast that poisons (emptiness of sleep: Combray i). Lime-flowers-Madeleine, the breast that satisfies (complete memory: Combray ii). Madeleine and lime-flowers are complementary foods (+ +). Sugary, calming, they are part of the series of good, nourishing objects of which the archetype, as we have seen, is "milk" (suckled cheek of the grandmother). Madeleine and tea, on the contrary, are foods bearing opposite signs (+ −), the location of an internal combat: being against non-being.

It's not surprising that this combat is "imagined" in the entire scene as a struggle between "memory" and "forgetfulness." A fantasy functions in a self-conscious text as it does in an oneiric formation. If the "madeleine," in the series of "good foods," acts as a substitution for "milk," the offer of the "madeleine and tea" is "*lait-thé*" (milk tea): "*Lethe*," River of Forgetfulness, joy of Nothingness. Without the help of memory, which the awakening sleeper experiences (1, 5), he would be lost in Nirvana, the ultimate extinction of the self in animal existence. The tea-madeleine, *lethal, is the mother who kills*. The lime-flowers-madeleine, the inoffensive and euphoric "filling-up," is the opposite: *the mother who has been killed*. Digested, assimilated, she is "transparent"; the narrator suddenly "rediscovers" the memory of himself, as if the living mother had been "blocking" it from him.

In what, then, does the unique strength of the new drink consist, and what are "lime-flowers" if we study them closely? Certainly, they are first (and foremost), in opposition to the Proustian series tea-coffee-alcohol, a tranquilizer: "Françoise would be making her tea; or, if my aunt were feeling 'upset,' she would ask instead for her 'tisane'" (1, 39). But this innocuous appearance is deceptive; "lime-flowers" quickly lose their innocence. As Germaine Brée perceptively brought to our attention, this description of the leaves' aging and drying out prefigures the final vision at the Guermantes' afternoon tea. The "lime-blossom experience" is already the last one in the *Temps retrouvé:* "These were indeed real lime-blossoms, like those I had seen, when coming from the train, in the Avenue de la Gare, altered, but only because they were not imitations but the very same blossoms, which had grown old" (1, 39). But the opposite is also true. If it may be said that the vision at the Guermantes' afternoon tea constitutes the sight of death written on people's faces, the contemplation of "this destructive action of

Time" (II, 1038), then the "lime-blossoms," harbinger of time, are also the harbinger of Death: "boiling infusion, in which she would relish the savour of dead or faded blossom" (I, 39). The signifier's ambiguity is pervasive: "These were petals which, before their flowering time, the chemist's package had embalmed on warm evenings of spring. That rosy candlelight was still their colour" (I, 39). The "lime-blossoms" are the mother's tomb, but one which she, like Lazarus, can leave, provided that the *feuilles* (leaves) be "dipped" in the infusion—recalling other "leaves" in which living creatures are stored, thanks to the pen "dipped" into another fluid.

The lime-flowers are, in sum, this strange herb found in the *Temps retrouvé:* "the cruel law of art that human beings should die and that we ourselves must die after exhausting the gamut of suffering so that the grass, not of oblivion but of eternal life, may grow, the thick grass of fecund works of art" (II, 1116). Herb of eternal *life*, the "lime-blossom" is the (textual; I, 47) source from which the Combraysian *Vivonne* flows. "Anti-tea," "*anti-Lethe*," the "lime-blossoms" are literature. In the form and color of the stems "twisted . . . into a fantastic trellis, in whose intervals the pale flowers opened" (I, 39), we recognize without doubt the "tiny crumbs of paper" of the Japanese game, those too in a bowl filled with water, which, "the moment they become wet, stretch themselves and bend, take on colour and distinctive shape, become flowers" (I, 36). Twisted, trellislike, with intervals, bent, efflorescent, this is the very *shape* of Proust's writing—but also the *color*. Recall Bergotte: "'That is how I ought to have written,' he said. 'My last books are too dry, I ought to have gone over them with several coats of paint, made my language exquisite in itself, like this little patch of yellow wall'" (II, 509). Bergotte's mistake is that he didn't put enough lime-flowers in his ink.

Despite the innocuous appearance of this detail (appearances, after all, are made for that), the substitution of lime-blossoms for tea constitutes the turning back upon the mother of the death impulse that has been directed against the son. This analysis is confirmed at the metonymic level by the fact that the famous sentence already discussed ("when from a long-distant past nothing subsists, *after the people are dead,*" etc.) slips in precisely between the moment when we do not yet know whether it is a question of "real or lime-flower tea" and the following paragraph where only lime-flowers "subsist," to use a Proustian term. The emergence of Death constitutes the elimination of the tea, the "bad object" representing the "bad mother." The "good object" causes the "good mother" to appear: Aunt Léonie replaces Mamma. If we may be permitted here to parody Lacan's formula according to which the symbolic father, insofar as he signifies the Law, is the dead father,[12] in Proust the "ideal mother," insofar as the Law has been subverted, is the "dead mother." The prohibition against incest, momentarily lifted by the debonair father himself in the prelude to the kiss scene ("tell Françoise to make up the big one for you, and stay beside him for the rest of the night" (1, 28), is hereafter formally eliminated. The "unique bed" that belongs to Aunt Léonie, the bed where she feels so well (so sick) that she never leaves it (1, 37), replaces the "two" beds from the bedtime scene.

The coherence of Proustian fantasy is complete; if it is true that the unconscious is really the "location" where we find an inflexible logic, where the original drama of the *Fort-Da* is experienced, where the tragedy of intermittent nourishment has left its trace, where the self becomes *lost* in the shadows of insomnia, then there too is it finally *found*—in *bed.* The location of the final anguish, to which fantasy clings from one end to the other of the *Recherche*, becomes the location of a mythical and mystical salvation through "transubstantiation," to use Proust's word. Finally possessing the "totality of his mother," which was always lacking—having "suckled" her to the point of exhaustive "assimilation," where nothing of the Other subsists except himself—the Narrator's ultimate desire is fulfilled through the most grievous of infractions against the Law. Through radical incestuous possession, which is not satisfied with the bliss of a banal Oedipal complex, he does not *have his mother*; he *is his mother.* He becomes himself by becoming her—in the beyond which is death. With the same stroke, metaphor comes into being; the "two" terms or "objects" are now "one," have completely coincided. Because if "Aunt Léonie" is the *dead mother*, "Aunt Léonie" is also *himself*.

◄ 8 ►

In this way, the formula for the Proustian unconscious, "To be yourself, you will become your own mother," leads to the fantasy, "I become my mother by becoming Aunt Léonie." A composite image, a double image, "Aunt Léonie" is produced through condensation, as in dream processes. The specific *caricatural* comedy attached to it recalls its psychic origin; it is marked by the ridicule that is its trademark. Despite the elaboration, the mother's face is visible beneath the aunt's disfigured features. Food/sleep: Aunt Léonie revolves around the two neurotic axes we have distinguished. Provider of food *for other people*—"they must be hungry!" (I, 103); she has to "make them veal," etc.—she herself *does not eat:* we are familiar enough with her "pepsin" and "Vichy water." The child puts his mother on a diet, in an imaginary reversal of roles: he *refuses* her the "food" that she gave him too much or too little of.

The punishment, moreover, is double, like the son's torment; the child *inflicts* upon her the *insomnia* he suffers and of which he complains to his mother (bedtime scene). In order to justify his genuine aggression, through a well-known projection device, he attributes aggression to the Other: "She was genuinely fond of us; she would have enjoyed the long luxury of weeping for our untimely decease" (I, 89). Even here, giving the adjective its full hostile value, a "disfigured" Mamma is clearly recognizable, inscribed in the Oedipal configuration. *Killing the father:* "And I've been dreaming that my poor Octave had come back to life" (I, 83). The return of the father constitutes an absolute nightmare, which waking up fortunately exorcises. The sexual meaning is underlined in a manner almost gross: Octave is resuscitated so that he can "make me take a walk every day" (I, 83). We can imagine the road he takes—*sleeping with his mother*. As we have indicated, this desire openly bears the Proustian stamp. To be fulfilled, it demands a funereal profanation. We have it when the Narrator donates "a big sofa," inherited from Aunt Léonie, to the keeper of a brothel: "Had I outraged the dead, I should not have suffered such remorse" (I, 440). This sofa, worthy counterpart to that upon which Mlle Vinteuil and her friend have it out, is distinguished by a noteworthy detail: "It was upon that same sofa that, many years before, I had tasted for the first time the sweets of love with one of my *girl cousins*" (I, 440). Here, it is very definitely in the family that this kind of thing is done.

But if Aunt Léonie is really the *projected mother* (what is bad has been expelled, nothing of the castrator remains), she is also the *introjected mother* (he appropriates all that is good). Without this double mechanism, the equation *Aunt Léonie = Mamma = me* would be impossible. The second mechanism is, moreover, attested to by Proust in the most explicit way: "Little by little, I was beginning to resemble all my relatives . . . I was becoming more and more like my Aunt Léonie" (II, 432). We owe the following remark to the strange *bedridden* state of the Narrator at the beginning of *La Prisonnière:* "A person (not Albertine, not any person that I loved, but a person with more power over me than any beloved) had *migrated into me* . . . my Aunt Léonie" (II, 432). Here, the "denial of love"—which is so obvious in the construction of the aunt figure, both at the manifest level of ridicule and at the level of the latent thoughts that we have seen at work—catches our attention less than the irresistible and bizarre "transmigration," which echoes in thousands of pages the "metempsychosis" discussed on the first page of the *Recherche*. The Proustian "self," so hotly pursued, remains forever locked in a system of successive possessions and dispossessions, as if the Narrator were "inhabited" by someone else. That Aunt Léonie is *him* as much as she is *Mamma* explains why the "punishment" inflicted upon the mother is noticeably "softened": if his aunt claims to be a martyr to insomnia, we nevertheless surprise her sleeping (I, 39) and even snoring (I, 83). Her dyspepsia is not so complete that she cannot try the "creamed eggs" (I, 43) or find strength in the "daily reappearance of those mashed potatoes" (I, 88). By striking his mother too hard in his aunt, our hero would hurt himself too much. For this reason, if his aunt has "renounced all earthly joys" (I, 43), hers is a gentle renunciation. Her ascesis is comfortable. Marcel-the-Aunt takes care of himself. Where does this "resemblance" come from? Why such an extraordinary "power" of enchantment on the part of such a colorless creature? Or, to translate Proustian terms into our language, what change does the mother undergo to become "léonized" in this way, so that she is from then on introjectable? The answer is in no way doubtful. Once again, "*l'idiot de la famille*" is the *writer*.

To begin with, Aunt Léonie is the *model mother:* far from subjecting the child to a system of constraints in which a battle for supremacy is fought, she contents herself with supervising her household, through the mediation of Françoise. Without bothering anyone, she assures everyone the satisfaction of all needs. She protects—from afar. She feeds—without indigestion. She is at others' disposal—without imposing herself. She governs—without ruling. The dead mother, resurrected, is the *mother-who-is-not-there*. Supremely discreet, she bequeaths her fortune, after death, without having given her love earlier, during her life: "My Aunt Léonie had bequeathed to me . . . almost all her unsettled estate—revealing thus after her death an affection for me which I had hardly suspected in her lifetime" (I, 348). In opposition to his grandmother, who loves the open air, who constantly "would come up and beg me to go outside" (I, 63), Aunt Léonie lets the child be; more specifically, she lets him read. Still more precisely, "I would be lying stretched out on my *bed*, a *book* in my hand, in my *room*" (I, 62).

Bed-book-room: again we find the familiar ingredients of the Proustian scene. But this time, instead of becoming alienated in a spoken reading in which the mother remains master of the language whose substance she appropriates, the child, through a silent retrieval of the word, *creates himself* in the realm of the imaginary; exactly, he *totalizes* himself in it: "This dim freshness of my room . . . presented to my imagination the entire panorama of summer, which my senses, if I had been out walking, could have tasted and enjoyed in fragments only" (I, 63). To the *piecemeal* pleasure of the real experience, the child prefers masturbatory pleasure (his words, his penis) as a *total* pleasure, at the expense of losing his reality in an *imaginary panorama*. The "omnipotence" of thought, where the self of the obsessional neurotic classically attempts to find himself or herself, is assured only in the reign of non-being: *to imagine* (in reading, well before writing) is to *settle permanently in death*. To settle in it is to *abolish* it, since it is equally true that death has effect only on the *real*. The privileged instants in which the Narrator ceases to feel "contingent" or "mortal" (masturbation, madeleine, court paving stones) constitute "this illusion, which brought close to me a moment from the past, incompatible with the present" (II, 996).

What Proust translates in terms of *temporality* ("even though the mere taste of a *madeleine* does not seem to contain logical justification for this joy, it is easy to understand that the word 'death' should have no meaning for him; situated outside of the *scope* of time, what could he fear from the future?"; II, 996) must be retranslated in terms of *reality*. What is situated "outside the scope of time" is not the "eternal"; it's the *unreal*. The Narrator's statement confirms this: "With the three memories of the past which had just come over me . . . instead of conceiving a more flattering idea of my inner self, I had, on the contrary nearly come to doubt the *present reality* of this self" (II, 997). At the three levels of the imaginary experience in which it is rendered—masturbation, memory, metaphor—this "joy" of "immortality" that flashes forth is in the end none other than the pleasure of something inane.

Now Aunt Léonie has made the inane the very texture of her life; she mimics it at every moment. In what we may call this "familial novel," which the Narrator invents, he creates a *model mother* for himself by creating her *on the model of himself*. Like God omnipotent, the writer creates for himself a mother in his own image—the writer-mother. Her stroke of genius is her "madness": this "mother who is never there" is, we say so appropriately, "in another world." Or, as we also say, she's "up in the clouds." Precisely—she lives "up there"; she "never comes down": "Aunt Léonie, who since her husband's (my uncle Octave's) death, had gradually declined to leave, first Combray, then her home in Combray, then her bedroom, and finally her bed; and who now never came down" (I, 37). This gradual and total withdrawal from the world—in another language, this generalized withdrawal of object libido, this universal disinvestment—is marked by a precise date: "I don't know what's become of my head since I lost my poor Octave" (I, 43). This "turning back of the libido upon the self," this "narcissistic regression," inducing a form of "dementia," is Aunt Léonie's wisdom, her *method*, in Hamlet's sense—*there is method in her madness*. Combray-home-bedroom-bed: a purely "anobjectal" libido is undoubtedly a myth. In any case, Aunt Léonie's entire strategy aims at disinvesting the world gradually in order to invest the *bed* totally.

To share your bed no longer with the Other is to be finally *chez vous*—to be yourself. Because in this bed, which you cannot share *with the Other* (bedtime scene, repeated with Albertine until we've had our fill of it) but in which you are never happy *without the Other* (Mamma or Albertine, whom you send for), all possibilities for happiness or unhappiness are gathered, "condensed," according to whether you can or cannot *fill it by yourself*. What the Narrator cannot do (opening of Combray I), Aunt Léonie can do, with a very special technique. Unable to abolish her needs, she *derealizes* them: she will eat without eating, sleep without being aware of it. "I must not forget that I never slept a wink" (I, 39). She transforms real sleep into fictional insomnia.

These exercises are essential but preliminary. The primordial need, of course, the one you have to eliminate in order to de-alienate yourself, is the need for the Other. But it's not enough for the Other to die for you to be free to be yourself. Dead or alive, the existence of the Other remains *real:* it is simply past or present. It's a question of making it *fictional*. Since the self can take shape only in the imaginary, in order to be yourself you have to *derealize other people*. The same device is applied to the needs of the self (to eat, to sleep) and to the need for the Other: you can satisfy a real need without subjecting yourself to it if you treat it like an imaginary need. Of course, in order to transform another person into fiction, you must first *derealize yourself*. "Aunt Léonie's system," set in place in this way, is in comic form none other than that which the Narrator selects in tragic form, at the end of a long ascesis.

The imaginary road is not smooth: in order to follow it to its end, you have to perform the exercises of a whirling dervish. Because to live in the imaginary, to challenge the reality principle, is normal in the child but pathogenic in the adult. It is a sickness. In order to live in the imaginary, you have to become an *imaginary invalid:* that is, to imagine a sickness. Sleeping well, digesting well, Aunt Léonie invents her insomnia and her dyspepsia. Robust, she can no longer move. At this point, this fictional "sickness" is only a false sickness, which a slip enables us to see through: "When in conversation she so far forgot herself as to say 'what made me wake up,' or 'I dreamed that,' she would flush and at once correct herself" (1, 39). Fiction here is deception. The *fiction must be true.* For that to be so, the imaginary invalid must be real. Aunt Léonie then adopts real behavior: doesn't go out, doesn't go down, stays in bed. This ˙generalized ankylosis in the end gives her true discomfort: "Sometimes a spell of fine weather made her a little more energetic, she would rise and put on her clothes; but before she had reached the outer room she would be 'tired' again and would insist on returning to her bed" (1, 110). "Somatizing" herself (just like Marcel, she suffers "chokings" and "other pains"; 1, 38), becomes true sickness, transforming the need for bed into a real need in which she remains subject to other people—the whole system collapses. To reestablish it, she must "psychize." An imaginary sickness can only be one that attacks the imagination. "I don't know what's become of my head" (1, 43). To be more exact: "She never spoke, save in low tones, because she believed that there was something broken in her head and floating loose there" (1, 39). When your brain is "cracked," what is floating free, naturally, is the "sense of reality." For Aunt Léonie the important thing is to believe (and to have others believe) that the moon is made of green cheese. "Batty," perhaps—Françoise *dixit*—she is not so foolish: pretending to take her neurosis for a psychosis, Aunt Léonie finds the right sickness: *simulated madness.* With that, you can't lose. Her know-how is knowing how to cheat without being routed. Because if the physical sickness is *real,* the true activity of the true invalid is the imaginary activity of a false madwoman. And if the sickness is *feigned,* the fictional activity of the false invalid becomes the real activity of a real madwoman. In both cases, you hit the mark. Through madness, true or false, the real passes into the unreal in a carefully closed circuit. By deliberately placing herself in the center of the whirligig, Aunt Léonie settles her being permanently in simulacrum. She doesn't eat, she doesn't sleep, she doesn't move; she no longer lives. She has brought about a radical transformation; her *real existence* is her *imaginary death*.

The "benefits" of the sickness, then, are obvious. Thanks to her false death, the aunt will possess all the rights of true dying persons regarding other people. She will exercise her tyranny. By dint of repeating, "The end is come at last, my poor Eulalie" (I, 53), without being believed, she has the craftsmen actually stop their work at Combray during her siesta. The imaginary invalid acquires real strength. It's not pure chance that the Narrator discovers this "transmigration" of Aunt Léonie in himself at the beginning of the *Prisonnière*. Their behavior is identical. By the price you pay for supposed suffering, you justify the privilege of inflicting true torment upon other people—whether it is Françoise, Eulalie, the kitchen girl, or Albertine. A clever weakness enables you to secure a relationship of power, to establish domination.

But the fundamental objective is not the real advantage that imaginary conduct acquires; the aim is the *imaginary treatment of the real*. The mother, of whose "practical wisdom, of what we would call nowadays the realism" (I, 29), the child is conscious, serves the reality principle exclusively. She refuses to yield to the nighttime blackmail of the kiss; she wants to cure her son of his "nervous disorder"; she does not hesitate to leave him, to go "to stay with my father," during the Balbec vacation (I, 492), or to leave him in Venice once the decision to go has been made (II, 837); she remains "anxious before all things that a definite rule of life should discipline the eccentricity of my nervous system" (I, 369). Such a *mother-reality*, in fact, bars the path of art; she is the *enemy of literature*. In the course of the Norpois dinner, where the taboo against a "career in letters" is removed, the mother unveils herself: "What she regretted was not so much seeing me abandon diplomacy as the prospect of my devoting myself to literature. But 'Let him alone!' my father protested; 'the main thing is that a man should find pleasure in his work'" (I, 369).

Father-pleasure yields for literature as he had for the bedtime scene. But the Narrator's identifications are feminine; more precisely, the primary identification remains with the mother, who alone can be *incorporated*. To satisfy his demands, which have been sufficiently analyzed, Proustian *fantasy* requires a *mother-pleasure*. Already, the "grandmother," produced through a scission of the maternal imago, has undergone the necessary transformation. In opposition to the "realistic" mother, she is by nature "ardently idealistic" (I, 29). Refusing all utilitarianism, she is *on the true path of art:* "Instead of photographs of Chartres Cathedral," she prefers "to give me photographs of Chartres Cathedral after Corot" (I, 31). Although more receptive than "Mamma" to the Narrator's caprice, the idealistic "grandmother" is not yet ideal. At Combray or Balbec, partial to walking, wanting to force him to go out, she remains overly caught up in exterior reality.

It's at this point that the fantasy causes Aunt Léonie to emerge: she will be *mother-pleasure*, the one who is *totally incorporable*. The substitution of Aunt Léonie for Mamma in the madeleine scene constitutes the replacement of a Mamma-madeleine (who cannot be assimilated, because she is real) by a *Léonie-madeleine* (who can be totally absorbed, because she is imaginary). By becoming Aunt Léonie, the Narrator appropriates not only maternal substance (substantial infantile regression, through her image); he incorporates the whole world, *everything real, which he dissolves in his thoughts.*

Here we see with remarkable precision how the most subtle literary theories are articulated in the most primitive fantasies. The role of the fantasy, in "producing" Aunt Léonie as conclusion to the madeleine scene, is to produce Proustian literature. Because Aunt Léonie, at the cost of wasting away her life, offers an extraordinary machine for derealizing (denying) the real. "From time to time, to add an interest to her life," Aunt Léonie introduces into it imaginary "minor complications, which she would follow up with passion" (I, 89). By becoming the Madwoman of Combray, she transforms her existence into "counterpane dramas" (1, 89). We have already seen the child enjoy an *imaginary panorama* (he too in a bed and in a bedroom) through reading. Between the two *spectacles*,[13] however, there is a qualitative difference. While reading *realizes the unreal*, the aunt does the opposite: she *derealizes the real*.

Each of the two operations possesses a distinct significance. As the author of "Journées de lecture" emphasizes in *Pastiches et mélanges*,[14] reading—superior to "conversation," which alienates us—consists in "having someone else's thought communicated to you while nevertheless remaining alone" (p. 226). The act of reading, however, can in turn become a form of alienation and thus "dangerous," "when, instead of wakening us to the personal life of the mind, reading tends to substitute itself for the former" (p. 234). But ultimately, "having someone else's thought communicated to you," is still to reenter the "nutritive" circuit. Food is this time spiritual to no avail; on the contrary, it makes you no less dependent upon the Other. The "spectacle" in books, if I may say so, is a *passive activity*. You create fantasies using someone else's scenario. The "counterpane dramas" that Aunt Léonie invents are, on the contrary, an *active passivity*. She creates fantasies using her own scenario; she creates autofantasies. We are very familiar with her schema. If the aunt transmigrates into him, in return the Narrator transfers his fantasy to her. The great "preoccupations" that pass through Aunt Léonie's life, her "great matters," are—as for the child of Combray—the rituals of food and sleep. As for the nature of the "spectacles" she enjoys (is that Mr. Pupin's daughter who is passing or not? is it going to rain or not? did Mrs. Goupil arrive at church before the elevation or after? etc.), we notice that it's always a question of determining a presence or an absence. Another form of this is marking an identity: was an unknown man seen near the *Pont-Vieux*? did an unknown dog pass by? In every case, it's a question of mastering the anxiety-producing effect of incomprehensible appearances and disappearances. Late in life, Aunt Léonie still plays the infantile game of *Fort-Da*.

The distance between nephew and aunt does not seem great. Metonymically, Aunt Léonie is part of the same narrative syntagma as the child of Combray 1; she is exactly contiguous to him. Meta-phorically, they seem even closer, because he is she. Yet an impor-tant gap exists. The "aunt" here is ahead of the "child"—or, rather, the fantasy is ahead of the work. If "Aunt Léonie" is still the child of Combray 1 in the throes of the infantile torment that we have de-scribed and that she tries to master, although the end is the same, the means are different. While the torment of absence in the child produces conduct that tends to make the real mother reappear, the play of appearances and disappearances in the aunt *produces* lan-guage. The "counterpane drama" is less a dramatic production than a verbal one:

In the next room, I could hear my aunt talking quietly to her-self. . . . she never remained for long, even when alone, without say-ing something . . . in the life of complete inertia which she led, she attached to the least of her sensations an extraordinary importance, endowed them with a Protean ubiquity which made it difficult for her to keep them secret, and, failing a confidant to whom she might communicate them, she used to promulgate them to herself in an unceasing monologue which was her sole form of activity. [1, 38–39]

The passivity of existence ("the life of inertia which she led") produces the incessant activity of a language. Cut off, transcending the world, the current of sensations flows over into waves of words. In the absence of the Other, speaker becomes listener in soliloquy. This verbal solipsism becomes the model for ipseity. Undiscover-able in the order of the real and of the imaginary, it is affirmed in the symbolic order: I am *me* while "talking to myself." Unfortu-nately, however, "sometimes . . . even these counterpane dramas would not satisfy my aunt" (1, 89). Even in the absence of the lis-tener, speech is a discourse for the Other, a call to him or her. It's "failing a confidant" that you speak to yourself. *Monologue* is a lack.

Suddenly the aunt invents *dialogue*: "she must see her work staged" (1, 89). Of course, as in the theater, real actors are needed: "And so, on a Sunday, with all the doors mysteriously closed, she would confide in Eulalie her doubts of Françoise's integrity and her determination to be rid of her, and on another day she would confide in Françoise her suspicions of the disloyalty of Eulalie, to whom the front-door would very soon be closed for good" (I, 89). "Closed" doors (of the room), "closed" and locked "front-door" (of the set): Aunt Léonie performs *her* "play/room." It's a play of *confinement*. With the *real* feelings of the actors (Françoise's and Eulalie's hostility) as the point of departure, she constructs an *imaginary* situation (she has no intention of getting rid of Françoise or of turning away Eulalie) with *fictional* characters (the unfaithful Eulalie, the pilfering Françoise). The performance would be incomplete, however, if the aunt herself did not take part in it; she needs to have her own role in her own "representation" (I, 89). Out of her real attitudes toward people, which she plays up at will ("the suspicions which Eulalie might occasionally breed in her were no more than a fire of straw," in contrast to those which she felt toward Françoise, "of whose presence under the same roof as herself my aunt was perpetually conscious"; I, 89–90), Aunt Léonie creates the imaginary role of a suspicious monarch. If certain "madmen" take themselves for Napoleon, she takes herself for Louis XIV; she "was able, too, to persuade herself that her silence, a shade of good humor or of arrogance on her features, would provide Françoise with matter for a mental commentary as tense with passion and terror, as did the silence, the good humor or the arrogance of the king . . . at Versailles" (I, 91). Of course, it is still power relationships, desire for domination, which are thus projected from the Other Stage onto this stage, but they are adapted for fiction: that is, for the only form in which they are capable of absolute actualization.

By instituting the reign of the *actual imaginary*, the aunt is ahead of the nephew—the fantasy is ahead of the work to come. By substituting their "images" for the "beings," she in effect carries out the work of the *novelist*: "The ingenuity of the first novelist lay in his understanding that, as the *picture* was the one essential element in the complicated structure of our emotions, so that simplification of it which consisted in the suppression, *pure and simple*, of 'real' people would be a decided improvement" (I, 64).

The novelist here, of course, is the Proustian novelist. If the analysis of the Narrator's relationship to the real mother enables us to ascertain the particular meaning that *writing* takes on in Proust, the analysis of the relationship to the phantasmatic mother enables us to "generate" the *novel*. In its *form*—the Narrator's uninterrupted "monologue" cut up by "dialogues"—the Proustian narrative is actually this *discourse* that replaces the classical *story*, which is precisely digested by an articulating instance that retrieves for its own benefit the terms of its own articulation (the "hero's" words) as if they were the articulation of the Other (the character's words). How could we not see the precise source of this solipsism, taking the form of soliloquy, in the incessant and autistic flow of language that the child-aunt keeps up by herself in bed? This source is acknowledged from the first sentence of the *Recherche:* "For a long time I used to go to bed early." From then on, speech passes for *Bed Discourse* (this bed where the Narrator will write); the narrative thus constituted under the original affect of the *Fort-Da* presents itself as a series of instantaneous appearances-disappearances of "characters," who "reappear" to "disappear" once again, without your ever being able to follow their trace completely.

The system of narrative discontinuities that structure the Proustian novel develops out of this fundamental intermittence. *Structure*, then, is not a simple technical choice. This "technique" enables the Narrator to master his deep anxiety vis-à-vis the inexplicable coming and going of the Other, while leaving intact the Other's arbitrary and lacunal quality, while respecting those very "gaps" that he himself—as the "hero" of the story—tries in vain to fill up. The writer, then, strives for the liberation which the whole book shows to be constantly escaping our grasp.

If it is true, according to the famous formula, that the *"matière"* of the Narrator's experience is the *"matière"* of his book (Pléiade III, 915), it is no less true that the structure of this experience gives the book its structure. Since the original experience is the absence of the Other, the self erects defense mechanisms, the total of which also compose the novel. "Whereas I had sought great laws, they called me one who grabs for petty details" (II, 1118). This double postulate on Proustian narration is a double defense reaction. Or rather, through jealous investigating, the Narrator will try by accumulating *details* to fill in those "huge intervals quite blank" that he mentions in reference to Albertine (II, 446) and into which he transposes the emptiness of "those inaccessible and torturing hours" when his mother has "gone to taste the unknown pleasures" (I, 24). These hours are a kind of strange "party" during which the woman you love slips away and which, we are appropriately told, Swann had experienced (I, 24). Let us note for those partisans of the "primal scene" the obvious meaning of the famous episode in which Swann peeks through Odette's window, a model for all future "jealousy." The infinite detail of Proustian writing, its untiring enumeration, its sentences which are constantly pursued or, rather, which constantly pursue further the obsession with imprisoning objects in metaphorical "rings"—this writing does not "reflect" nor does it "wed" jealousy's movements; it *is* jealousy. According to the noteworthy analysis in *Jean Santeuil:* "love, which . . . awakens through the medium of jealousy . . . a wild curiosity . . to know every detail of what she is doing . . . turned . . . a fragment of her secret life, a hitherto concealed page of an actuality . . . into something of such enormous interest."[15]

For the writer-translator, to write is to relocate-the-unlocatable-page. A metaphor for writing, on the thematic level the obsessional "jealousy" scene, in the privileged form of spying and voyeurism (Montjouvain, Charlus and Jupien, Saint-Loup's staircase, brothel peephole, etc.), offers a kind of caricature of the narrative impulse. This "scene" structures all the *forms of the appearance of the Other,* which have been studied and catalogued by Gaëtan Picon. Moreover, Aunt Léonie, here in her relationship with Françoise, already presents the model: "and so on by degrees, until her mind had no other occupation than to attempt, at every hour of the day, to discover what was being done, what was being concealed from her by Françoise. She would detect the most furtive movement of Françoise's features, something contradictory in what she was saying, some desire which she appeared to be screening" (I, 90).

If we feel we have already found the description of the relationship between the Narrator and Albertine or, more generally, of that between the Proustian novelist and his characters, it should not surprise us, since what we discover in the hardly veiled form of the projection mechanism are the feelings and behavior of the Narrator vis-à-vis his mother.

Yet as the Narrator discovers in a long and painful apprenticeship (this is perhaps what is essential in what he learns in this *Bildungsroman*), however voluminous the sum total of our information may be, it never amounts to an adequate, let alone complete, knowledge; the other person remains an enigma. The "huge intervals quite blank" are not filled by specific knowledge. The contrary defense, which Picon's analysis accurately defines, must be put into play: "A mechanism of reduction which links the individual appearance to a notion, a precedent, a law, opposes this appearance."[16] The other aspect, the other vocation in the *Recherche*, is given here: the search for "great laws," the law of deception by the real, of love's illusions, implacable laws that regulate the snob's behavior as well as the liar's, etc. This is the famous Proust of "maxims" (with which criticism entertained itself by collecting them as a source of knowledge); the Proust with a "pessimistic psychology" (which is connected to the "pessimism" of "classicists" of the purest tradition); the Proust, finally, of an "analysis" that is logical, sinuous, lacking metaphorical ornament. We find this in the *Prisonnière* and the *Fugitive*, and also to a degree everywhere else. "Aunt Léonie" sheds some precious light once again on this Proust: an *unknown* man near the Pont-Vieux, a passing dog that she *doesn't know*—her rapid intervention reduces the *unknown* to the *known*, causes the mystery of unusual "appearances" to reenter the system of Combray's "laws."

Such is the Narrator's obsession as well—which is why he demands, for "the necessary rings of a beautiful style," the same rigorous statute as for "the sole relationship in the world of science, the law of cause and effect" (II, 1008). If it is impossible to seize the Other in the totality of specific knowledge, you rid yourself of this irreducible existence by dissolving it in the *generality of a law*. It is in fact this end that literature serves as well: "If he has finally achieved his true vocation, during the hours of work, he feels so clearly the loved one *merge* into a vaster reality" (II, 1019–20). The dissolving action of law has already begun in language's abstractions: "to transcribe . . . into a universal language" (II, 1019) an individual existence is to preserve only its essence. If "a book is a great cemetery" (II, 1018), it's because by the very nature of doing so, to put into words is to put to death. In this regard, Mallarmé is particularly sensitive to the absence of the thing in the word; Proust, not without a guilty conscience and remorse (II, 1018), gives special emphasis to the disappearance of beings in the language which is supposed to resurrect them. This remorse is understandable: filial remorse is the gravedigger in this cemetery. The guilty conscience has a different origin: it's the writer's bad faith; this "individuality," which he refuses to the Other as the object in language, is reserved for himself as the subject, the "author." The law of "merging" works one way only: in the very place that other beings become lost, the artist finds his irreducible difference. From this point of view, the *Recherche* formula might be "others die, so that I may rise from my death."

The "science" of Proustian writing is a false science. Whereas the true scholar destroys himself, as a separate existence, in the order of the law he institutes, the Narrator forms a kind of enclave in the system of his "laws"; he grants himself the status of extra-territoriality. Laws are made for other people. The writer is a swindler. Not, of course, that he does not, as a *man*, reenter "psychological law": erotic fantasy, amorous fancies, worldly illusions— he subsumes himself within his own categories. But just as Aunt Léonie, by settling herself at the center of her whirligig, claims to remain mistress of the imaginary game, to exit unhurt from it in the end, the Narrator merges the "hero's" being with a universal order only to better fuse it once again to himself. "Madame knows everything; Madame is worse than the X-rays" (I, 41). Like aunt, like nephew: "I did not see the guests, because, when I thought I was looking at them, I was looking through them as with an X-ray" (II, 888).

This "X-ray" glance, which grasps the "true"—that is, the general in the individual, the law in the event—strips the Other of being. Penetrated by the light of day, others are phantoms—in more precise terms, "fantasies." Between the moment when the narrator leans over Albertine's neck and the moment when he kisses her, ten Albertines appear in succession. The Albertines in this "series," moreover, do not meet: the one in Balbec I, in Paris, in Balbec II, in the Parisian prison, the dead one—these fragments remain disparate forever. Rome is no longer in Rome, it is wherever I am. So it is with Albertine, or with anyone: "Our social personality is created by the thoughts of other people" (I, 15). So is our private personality. At the end of the "X-ray," the Proustian diagnostic constitutes a certificate that recognizes the nonexistence of the Other.

Inversely, as the madeleine experience shows, the Narrator himself *exists*. Triumphing over the law of disappearance of the causal order, his defunct "self" suddenly attaches itself to him once again. By this means, no longer "contingent" and "mortal," he is the exception that confirms the rule. To be more exact, he is the exceptional being, because through this exception *he has being*.

We haven't left our "madeleine"; the Narrator doesn't leave it for a second. At the beginning of the *Recherche*, for the child, *the Other has being, so I don't have it*. At the end of the *Recherche*, for the writer, *I have being, so others don't have it*. The whole course of writing is at stake here, in the reversal of a *fantasy*. The writer is the Thief of Being. Proustian space lays itself out here, in Aunt Léonie's "madness." Proustian "reasoning," the "analysis" of feelings, the tirelessly repeated "laws" are only reiterations of the obsession— symptomatic ratiocinations where the scholarly surface, upon close examination, often masks contradictions and absurdities. Clinical mania constitutes the ultimate, subtle refuge of derangement. This is, in fact, why that part of the work in which the logical obsessions of a theorizing discourse culminate (the *Prisonnière* and the *Fugitive*) is exactly the part where—after Aunt Léonie has finally "transmigrated" into him, has finally established her "system" in him—the Narrator, withdrawn and bedridden, reaches the height of his delirium.

◄ 9 ►

Let's suspend the analysis for a minute; "terminated," "interminable," as always, stopping it constitutes a brutal arrest, because the fantasy itself does not stop structuring the work. But it also *deconstructs* what it *constructs*, in continual reversals of meaning. The writer steals being in order to offer it in the universal domain of language. He kills, to resurrect. "The true life . . . is literature." The real is completely emptied and preserved in the tomb of the symbolic. But this salvation is nevertheless of an imaginary order. The original murder, by means of which the book is instituted, can turn back upon it. The death wish, which had previously turned against the writer, in the end turns against writing.

We are familiar with the vision through which "Bergotte was not dead for ever and ever": "They buried him, but all through the night of mourning, in the lighted windows, his books arranged three by three kept watch like angels with outspread wings and seemed, for him who was no more, the symbol of his resurrection" (II, 510). But this edifying assumption is demystified in advance: "Heat will withdraw from the earth, then life itself. Then the resurrection will have come to an end, for if, among future generations, the works of men are to shine, there must first of all be men. . . . and if we suppose Bergotte's fame to have lasted so long, suddenly it will be extinguished for all time" (II, 507).

But we don't need to wait for a distant end of the world by entropy. For himself, the Narrator is less generous than for Bergotte: "Doubtless my books also, like my earthly being, would finally some day die. But one must resign oneself to the idea of death. One accepts the idea that in ten years one's self, and, in a hundred years one's books, will no longer exist. Eternal existence is not promised to books any more than to men" (II, 1120). At the very moment when literature, having attained full consciousness, assigns to man "a place . . . extending boundlessly . . . in Time" (II, 1124), the statute of literature abolishes the last words of the work in advance.

In addition, in his study of "Proust palimpseste," Genette has indeed shown that Proustian metaphor, theoretically destined to indicate the essence common to two objects, in fact functions as a twirling of appearances: the sea is described in terms of a mountain, the mountain as a sea, etc.[17] Instead of a unique relation we have perpetual returns, a whirligig of opposites. The "minute released from the chronological order of time" (II, 997) does not escape this structure: "This illusion which brought close to me a moment from the past, incompatible with the present, never lasted any length of time" (II, 996).

Metaphor, which was supposed to arrest vertigo, succumbs to it. We understand how Genette can say of Proustian writing that "intending to indicate essences, it winds up constituting, or restoring, mirages" (p. 52). I must say that Aunt Léonie has charmed Proust. The phantasmic identification that has "made" the text, "unmakes" it. Once you have entered the imaginary system, you can no longer leave—even through death. Aunt Léonie has settled her real life in an imaginary death so well that even her true death, when it occurs, remains *fiction:* "She had died at last, leaving both parties among her neighbors triumphant in the fact of her demise—those who had insisted that her mode of life was enfeebling and must ultimately kill her, *and, equally,* those who had always maintained that she suffered from some disease not imaginary but organic" (I, 117).

By dint of "derealizing" the real, fantasy ends up "derealizing" the imaginary, which begins again within the network of the real, because what survives at the end of the phantasmatic process by which the murdered mother comes back to life as the ideal mother (the writer-son) is the *ambivalence conflict,* pure and simple, which the act of writing was supposed to overcome. "Died at last": the death wish, twice displayed—from the real mother to the fictional mother, and from the level of affective doubt to that of "objective" hypothesis ("imaginary or organic" illness)—is fulfilled in vain; it remains locked within an insoluble, conflictual structure. An irreducible opposition remains as in the case of the conflicting views of both groups of neighbors. The euphoric "digestion" of the mother and the "complete assimilation" of the other person are myths: $1 + 1$ makes 2, and not 1. The "two objects" that are distinct are not reabsorbed into a "common essence"; the "two terms" that are distinct are not connected by "the only true relationship." The dream of symbiosis and the folly of metaphor (whose close relation we have already seen) disappear all at once. Ontological unicity and metaphoric unity are equally impossible. Opposites endure, their union is only an "illusion," in the domain of memory or of writing, which lasts only as long as an attack of vertigo—an illusion created by the momentary flutter of signifiers, whether they be words or images.

What is true of writing is, at the other end, also true of reading. Without intending to prolong indefinitely this study of the Proustian text, we must, however, point out that reading shares in the same impossible wish, in the same unrealizable structure. Whereas reading aloud affirms a duality, solitary reading is an act of identity. Proust's theoretical definition of reading, "having someone else's thought communicated to you while nevertheless remaining alone," allows the danger of alienation to remain alive, as we have seen. Solitude is not solipsism: through a book, the Other can be transported into us, can live in us. Now as a writer, it's a question of turning to his advantage the alienation that he fears as a reader. He must retrieve in advance the inevitable "otherness" of reading, "assimilate" and "digest" it. The last "theory of reading" is constructed along these lines: "In reality, each reader reads only what is already within himself" (II, 1024). The act of reading can establish that miraculous coincidence of self and Other that memory and metaphor have failed to offer: "It is this reading within himself what is also in the book which constitutes the proof of the accuracy of the latter and *vice versa*" (II, 1024). In this "sort of optical instrument" (II, 1024), the person looking and the person looked at become one and the same. Or—another Proustian metaphor—the "mirror" of the book can, in effect, cause parallel rays to converge in a single center.

But in speaking of optics, of course, it's a question of an *illusion*. The fusion of images is a delusion; the pure identity of alter ego and ego is folly. He (the artist) alone expresses things *for others* and seeks to reveal them to themselves (II, 1079). It is the writer who "translates" and "deciphers" deceptive appearances *for the Other* (II, 1080). In this new form of symbiosis, which it is now the turn of writing to assume, the reader is only the child, the parasite. In the instance that "nourishes," the mother, the master, is the author. Reading becomes a trap to "catch the Other," a strategy to reverse once again, in the imaginary, the roles of the real domination. Once again, however, an imaginary supremacy continues to be a fictional superiority. An opposite is produced; the one who thought he was doing the catching is caught: "It was sad for me to think that my love, which had meant so much to me, would be so detached in my book from any person that different readers would make it apply closely to the love they had felt for other women" (II, 1018). In this "posthumous infidelity" (II, 1018), whatever he does to console himself, the cuckold is the writer. No matter how prodigious his trap of words, the *alter ego* who reads is never the *ego* who writes. Even if he offers himself, the one who reads you is *at one and the same time* "you" and "he." The separation remains absolute, the ambivalence stays intact. The reader is no more "edible" than Albertine or Mamma.

Love, memory, writing, reading: along the major axes of the *Recherche*, the fusion of differences is a momentary confusion; the two-in-one is only illusion; the quest for identity is vertigo. It's normal that the Narrator, having conceived such an enterprise, should fall victim to a dizzy spell (II, 1117). The childhood dream is impossible: *the real cannot be incorporated in the imaginary.* Or, if you will: *that cannot be eaten.* It is in this sense that "Aunt Léonie" and her "madeleine"—beatific introjection of the "good object" and the "good mother"—that make the *Recherche* emerge, also veil its ultimate truth. Torn apart, the material of the fantasy returns Proust's work to its very impossibility. Unresolved ambivalence continues to make the book revolve in the dizzying counterpoint of its perpetual reversals.

The internal logic of the fantasy unceasingly structures the text's movement. It deconstructs what it constructs—it's Proust's *perpetuum mobile*—but does so in order to reconstruct, beyond Proust. It is hard to leave "Aunt Léonie" without pointing out a curious phenomenon. Like those Proustian characters who die and come back to life after a one-page digression, Aunt Léonie dies in Proust only to live again elsewhere. A withdrawal from the world; reclusion in a house, then in a bedroom, in a bed she no longer leaves; gradual loss of physical and mental faculties; sickness that

rible truth, my mother's image sometimes mingles with theirs";
p. 59) —an episode in which, if our analysis of Proust is correct, we
find in the features of the poisoning mother a kind of caricatured
Beckettian variant of the "madeleine": "So I will only add that this
woman went on giving me slow poison, slipping I know not what
poisons into the drink she gave me, or into the food she gave me, or
both, or one day one, the next the other" (p. 53). That these "poisons," which Mother-Circe combines with eating and drinking, can
evoke the "madeleine" will appear less surprising when we learn
that it is a question of Lousse's "*molys*" (p. 54) —mythological
food, which is stamped like that of Proust by the initial of the
m(aternal) signifier and in which a name filiation from "Molloy"
can be read. Of course, it is not at all a question of trying to establish one of those "literary influences" that made up the good old
days of criticism, but of observing the operation of a fantasy from
text to text. The theoretical explanation is of little importance
here: a universal fantasy, of which both texts would constitute individual "variants," or perhaps a sociocultural complex localized
in history (both kinds of explanations are probably complementary and necessary). I would simply like to indicate the curious
progression of a kind of "phantasmatic transtextuality," if you will
allow me this expression.

Impossible identification with his mother produces Molloy's
wanderings as it determines the long itinerary of the Narrator
of the *Recherche*. Given this, the family resemblances we unex-
pectedly discover between Proust's autobiographical projection
and Beckett's fantastic ectoplasm are not a matter of chance. At a
superficial level, certain anecdotal parallels strike us immediately.
Sharing, among other afflictions, the Narrator's asthma crises ("Ah
yes, my asthma. . . . The noise betrayed me, I turned purple. It
came on mostly at night"; p. 79), Molloy has some of his surprising
habits ("I sleep little and that little by day"; p. 14) —and not only
in matters of health. Confronting the fundamental ambiguity of
sex, a prisoner of Lousse about whom he wonders "if she was not a
man rather or at least an androgyne" (p. 56), Molloy gives free
reign to the anal, repressed by Proust's Narrator and displaced upon

little by little moves in and overcomes her entire being; general paralysis in which the only remaining sign of life for the eye is furtive glances out the window, for the tongue is the "unceasing monologue which was her sole form of activity," for the mind is "the habit of thinking aloud" (I, 39). What survives in the head, condemned in this way to slow extinction? "Something broken in her head and floating loose there, which she might displace by talking too loud" (I, 38). Who doesn't see that beyond Proust, *Aunt Léonie gives birth to Beckett?*

It's no surprise that Beckett's first book is a *Proust* (long "repressed" in English and still "prohibited" in French, as if Proust's murder of the parental instance had to be replayed!). This ambivalent homage is, after all, the least of it. Here is Molloy:

> *I am in my mother's room. It's I who live there now . . . I sleep in her bed. I piss and shit in her pot. I have taken her place. I must resemble her more and more. . . .*
>
> *Yes, so far as I was capable of being bent on anything all of a lifetime long, and what a lifetime, I had been bent on settling this matter between my mother and me, but had not succeeded. . . .*
>
> *And of myself, all my life, I think I had been going to my mother, with the purpose of establishing our relations on a less precarious footing. And when I was with her, and I often succeeded, I left her without having done anything. And when I was no longer with her I was again on my way to her, hoping to do better the next time.*[18]

You don't have to look for the Penelope for whom Beckett's Ulysses feels impossible nostalgia—whom he tries to go back to at the end of his reptations or in the soliloquy of his paralysis, but whom he finds again in vain, only to leave her once more. The source of attraction is balanced by a force of repulsion, or independent propulsion: "And far more than to know what town I was in, my haste was now to leave it, even were it the right one, where my mother had waited so long and perhaps was waiting still" (p. 65).

Reversal of the movement is underlined, in the burlesque mode, by the episode of deliverance from the completely maternal domination of "Circe-Lousse" ("And God forgive me, to tell you the hor-

Charlus, though he arrives at the same practical solution: "However. Twixt finger and thumb 'tis heaven in comparison" (p. 58). The *mise-en-scène* of writing (seclusion, sickness, confinement to bed) advances to its final consequences a process begun in the *Prisonnière*, on the model of the aunt. At Aunt Léonie's window, we do not fail to find Molloy once again: "In my head there are several windows, that I do know, but perhaps it is always the same one, open variously on the parading universe. The house was fixed, that is perhaps what I mean by these different rooms" (p. 51). In going from the multiple exterior similes to the deep structure of the experience that produces them, we find very quickly in Molloy the equivalent of the Narrator's traumatic depersonalization through sleep upon which the *Recherche* opens and is built:

And it came back also to my mind, as sleep stole over it again, that my nights were moonless and the moon foreign to my nights, so that I had never seen, drifting past the window, carrying me back to other nights, other moons, this moon I had just seen, I had forgotten who I was (excusably) and spoken of myself as I would have of another. . . . Yes it sometimes happens and will sometime happen again that I forget who I am and strut before my eyes, like a stranger. [p. 42]

If the two texts are literally and semantically superimposable, it is because, in both cases, the experience of sleep is indicative of a more fundamental experience of loss of self, of internal schism of the ego in which the ego grasps itself irremediably as Other. Starting out from identical premises, Molloy advances further than the Narrator. The solidity of the waking state can no longer be distinguished from the fluidity of sleep ("For my waking was a kind of sleeping"; p. 53). There is no longer any room for a Proustian recovery of the self from the moment when, according to a remarkable formula, you happen not only to forget who you are but also to forget to be ("Yes, there were times when I forgot not only who I was, but that I was, forgot to be"; p. 49). Proustian fantasy, turned back upon itself (the impossibility of rejoining being in the mother, but the reciprocal impossibility of finding any being in the self) will finally break open Proust's narrativity. Whereas in the *Recherche* the desire to have the self and the Other coincide, the obsession with the fusion of differences, will establish at the narrative level the symbiosis of the *two-in-one* ("I" reference and "I" referent, "hero" and "Narrator" are, after all, *the same*), the insurmountable cleavage of the self in Beckett will produce the explosion of the narrative instance. "Molloy" becomes "Moran" (but perhaps it's not the same; perhaps the same is *the Other*); the Proustian "two-in-one" (I/I) becomes the *one-in-two* of the Beckettian break (Molloy/Moran).

The reading of the fantasy, however, is by no means a one-way thing; it is written in the alternating signs of the boustrophedon. We proceeded from Proust to Beckett; the opposite is just as valid, and this insistent and bizarre "brotherhood" is legible in both directions. If the Beckettian cripple has become a paradigm for us, if we are accustomed to seeing him lose one of his bodily attributes from play to play, and to strip himself of all human appearances from novel to novel, we are less prepared to find in Proust an anticipated model of literal decomposition. In "transmigrating" into the Narrator, Aunt Léonie is not content with making a simple valetudinarian out of him, a calm patient settled in a comfortable neurosis. She enters him as others are put out—with loss and with a crash, so to speak.

Crash: "Three times I nearly *fell* as I went down the stairs. . . . I felt as though I had become incapable of anything, as frequently happens to an old man who, active the day before, *breaks his hip* or has an attack of indigestion and may for some time to come lead a bedridden existence which is only a more or less long preparation for the now inevitable end" (II, 1117).

Loss: "Illness had exhausted my mental faculties and (as I had noticed long before) . . . the power of my memory" (II, 1122). "Those hours after which, my tongue paralysed, as was the case with my grandmother during her last illness, I would no longer be able to utter a word" (II, 1118).

Loss of memory, of language, following a peculiar accident: a *fall*—who doesn't see the fundamental elements of Beckettian symbolism? What is more, Proustian writing does not belong to the "early sickness." Anguish, choking, asthma, insomnia, weakness leave the recluse every opportunity *to talk* about literature in a scholarly way with Albertine, but do not allow him *to write*. It's the accident on the stairway which, taking speech away, will liberate writing.

If, in fact, the illumination brought about by the "court paving stones" and the meditation that follows in the Guermantes' library constitute the moment of *conception* of the work, there remains before its *realization* a final stage to cross, which, unless I am mistaken, criticism has hardly noticed. It's simply that Aunt Léonie's "neurosis" must occur, must become authentic, in the Narrator. The imaginary death must become *the beginning of an actual death*. This "strange thing which occurred" on the stairway (II, 1117) is nothing less than the radical break that transforms the imaginary invalid into a dying man. We have to reread this extraordinary passage, which can serve as an afterword to Proust's work and as a preface to Beckett's:

I do not think that, on the day I became half-dead, it was the accompanying symptoms, such as my inability to descend the staircase, to recall a name, to get up, which gave rise, even by an unconscious process of reasoning, to the idea of death, the idea that I was already nearly dead, but rather that all this had come at the same time, that inevitably the great mirror of the mind was reflecting a new reality. [II, 1120]

This "new reality" is indeed a death that is *real*, no longer acted out or performed as a series of symptoms. We must be aware that writing in Proust does not burst forth from a joyful being at his strongest, as we like to think is the case for a Hugo, a Claudel, or a Goethe—those "Olympians" of literature; rather, it is lodged in the gradual loss of being. The Narrator doesn't write, according to the time-honored expression, "at the height of his powers" but suffering from *their loss*, trying to compensate for it: "The loss of my memory aided me a little by cutting out some of my obligations; my work filled their place" (II, 1119). The Proustian Narrator, then, writes *precisely* in a "Beckettian position." He composes while decomposing himself. *Le Temps retrouvé* closes in the way that *Molloy* opens: "What I'd like now is to speak of the things that are left, say my goodbyes, finish dying" (p. 7). Overflowing sentences, luxuriant metaphors, rich style overcompensate for extreme poverty, for a final deprivation. Proustian excess masks a lack. Hiding behind the showy facade, as is always the case with the baroque—*nothing*. The radical difference (personal and cultural, historical) between Proust and Beckett is that the second removes the veil that the first hangs. The end result of Proustian fantasy, its fulfillment in Beckett, is this: the invention of a writing that communicates, above all, a lack.

In the circuit of fantasy, if Proust *announces* Beckett, Beckett, in reverse, recalls and *denounces* Proust, whose latent meaning he reveals or, more precisely, whose meaning he "reworks" beyond the limits of an *oeuvre*. "Having a body constitutes the principle danger that threatens the mind" (II, 1114). Language begins to take shape when the body begins to die.

But what state is it to be "half-dead" or "already nearly dead," as the Narrator describes himself? "I felt as if I had no memory, no power to think, no strength, no life at all. . . . I would have let them do to me whatever they wished without uttering a word or opening my eyes" (II, 1117). "I craved nothing now but rest, while waiting for the long rest that would eventually come" (II, 1119).

In this final reversal, which is a reversion—in the way that we say the elderly man "returns to his childhood"—the dying man returns to the prenatal state. Passing through domains in the opposite direction, he goes back down from the human and from the animal to the vegetable: "I fell back exhausted, closed my eyes and for a week I merely vegetated" (II, 1118). Man returning to a crawl, fusing the larval and the telluric, is explicit in Molloy: "And I even crawled on my back plunging my crutches blindly behind me into the thickets, and with the black boughs for sky to my closing eyes. I was on my way to mother. And from time to time I said, Mother, to encourage me I suppose" (p. 90).

It is important here not to discover a modern illustration of the "archetypal" Earth Mother but to grasp its precise meaning for the writer. Beckett himself says it clearly, speaking of Proust: "The artistic tendency is not expansive, but a *contraction.*" We see the immediate consequence of this "contraction" of art: "And art is the apotheosis of solitude. There is no communication because there are no vehicles of communication."[19] We have seen a good deal of this contraction at work in Aunt Léonie's existence. A gradual withdrawal from the world sets the "model" in place. It's the "bedroom-bed-paralysis-monologue," which also becomes the Beckettian "model." It is directly linked to that of the dual relationship to the mother, which you never manage to leave behind or to go back to; from which you can neither free yourself nor separate yourself: insoluble conflict, producing contradictory behavior (adoration and profanation in sacrilegious gestures in Proust, obscene words in Beckett) and leading into a progressive inertia (bedroom-bed-paralysis).

The "monologue" articulated here is the language of this impossibility of living, which the long agony of dying mimics and which the operation of fantasy resolves on the imaginary level. In a preceding analysis, we spoke of infantile regression in the case of "Aunt Léonie." This regression is even greater: a return to the womb, already clearly glimpsed in the form of the "quite thin partition" separating the Narrator from his grandmother, upon which he has only to give "three knocks" to have her come to "give him milk." The moment of writing, anchored in death, takes up the same "material" and gives it a final dimension:

I made up my mind to waste in sending apologies to Mme. Mole and condolences to Mme. Sazerat one of those hours after which, my tongue paralysed, as was the case with my grandmother during her last illness, I would no longer be able to utter a word or even swallow some milk. . . . the remembrance of my work was vigilant and would employ in laying the first foundations the hour of extra existence which had thus reverted to me. [II, 1118]

Writing will function in place of the speech he has lost, in place of the dead mother. Ink is the resurrection of the milk. In the fantasy's logic, the dying writer writes in a fetal position: "Yes, when you can neither stand nor sit with comfort, you take refuge in the horizontal, like a child in its mother's lap" (*Molloy*, 140).

Thus a more subdued light is cast upon the well-known sentence: "The only true paradise is always the paradise we have lost" (II, 994), a sentence that lies at the very heart of the experience of the "past recaptured." It is a completely imaginary paradise, since it is *prior to the real*; extratemporal, since it is *prior to time*; escaping contingency and death, since it is *prior to birth*. By a final circuit of the fantasy, the actual entry into death becomes a refusal to enter into life.

"I had ceased now to feel mediocre, accidental, mortal. Whence could it have come to me, this all-powerful joy?" (I, 34). We can perhaps read the madeleine scene at an even more archaic level. If the Narrator's obsession is the quest for his lost being, he can find it only in the place where it was first given to him: in that "mother's lap" that Beckett talks about. Because, finally, what is the madeleine experience if not a kind of *déjà vu*—or, rather, a kind of *déjà senti*, already felt? And isn't the feeling of *déjà vu* constantly the pivot around which swing the jolts to the memory that mark the Proustian itinerary, from the Hudimesnil trees to the Guermantes court paving stones? Moreover, "occurrences of *déjà vu* in dreams have a special meaning. These places are invariably the genitals of the dreamer's mother."[20] It definitely has this meaning also in the text. Because the obsession with the *two-in-one*, with the $1 + 1 = 1$, which the Narrator projects in all his relationships with others, could only come from *there*, since it is fulfilled only *there*. The dual relationship is a second state or, rather, a second stage, which is already nostalgia for an original fusion, for a lost age, where *all* difference is abolished (beings: love; sensations: memory; signs: metaphor) and where Proust's deepest desire to write originates. Organ-that-feeds: below the rivalries and the ambivalence that occur after birth, which we have tried to reconstruct, the serenity of visceral enclosure is affirmed, the joy of the primitive circuit.

"I raised to my lips a spoonful of the tea in which I had soaked a morsel of the cake" (I, 34). Aunt Léonie "was able to dip in the boiling infusion . . . a little madeleine, of which she would hold out a piece to me when it was sufficiently soft" (I, 39). Madeleine which insists upon being "softened" by the fantasy in the "infusion": happiness of the embryo floating in its lime-flower-urine. "The same symbols which occur in their infantile aspect in bladder dreams, appear with an eminently sexual meaning in their 'recent aspects': water = urine = semen = amniotic fluid" (*Interpretation of Dreams*, 439, n. 1). This symbolic movement, established by Rank, is certainly confirmed here in a specific variant: lime-flower = urine = sperm (masturbation, *Contre Sainte-Beuve*) = amniotic fluid (madeleine, *Recherche*)—which explains in an even more precise way why the two texts we have studied may be superimposed. They function in an equivalence equation.

But equivalence is not identity. In the symbolic chain, the madeleine is situated at a much deeper level, indicates a much more archaic fantasy than the adolescent masturbation scene. In this sense—and Proust as novelist is right—the madeleine scene is a narrative matrix (contrary to the first text), since it serves as the matrix for the fantasy of writing. If, in our treatment of the text as logograph, we said that the first offer of the *madeleine-tea* functioned, in the play of symbolic substitutions, as *lait-thé* (milk-tea) = *Lethe* (the mythological river cited by Proust; II, 116), we can better grasp *which waters* we must cross in order for this "exquisite pleasure" ("at once the vicissitudes of life had become indifferent to me, its disasters innocuous, it's brevity illusory"; I, 34) to project us outside of time.

Hence the eminently *positive* pleasure of the madeleine. But the path to paradise is infernal torture. We understand better that "having a body constitutes the principal danger that threatens the mind." If it is true, as Beckett says, that in Proust "the artistic tendency is not expansive, but a contraction," the drama lies in the fact that the spiritual law is one of involution, whereas the biological law is one of evolution. The body progresses when the spirit wants to regress. A new reversal comes to structure the *Recherche:* it is the narrative of a *life* that unfolds at the moment when it is folding back up again, in a *time* that unwinds by an act in which it winds up again. This is a contradiction that *writing* echoes, since criticism is always wondering whether the book we are reading, the "written" book, is the same as that which is "to be written." The future is a past; the present of the book is to deconstruct itself in the movement that constructs it. The same fantasy organizes all levels: *the true direction is the opposite direction;* that is, we move forward by moving backward. But no fetus wants this. As Beckett's Moran (parody of the Proustian Narrator; an "I" different from self to the point of being an Other) says, you return to the maternal bosom "when you can neither stand nor sit with comfort" (*Molloy*, 140).

If *to go toward death* is *to go toward birth, the birth (of the book)* is *the death (of its author)*. To recapture the lost paradise of the embryo demands a complete ascesis: rid yourself of the adult; strip away your arms and legs; lose all the attributes of corporeal independence; go back down the path of evolution. Such is the Law of Writing which the phantasmagoria of Beckettian mutilation represents, and which the Narrator incorporates in the series of hysterical conversions that culminate in the fall on the staircase.

This law of writing functions, however, in diametrically opposed ways in Proust and Beckett. Proust's writing is a mask; Beckett's, the mark of a lack. This must be understood in more specific terms: it is the lack of the subject. In effect, for Proust, the equation "to go toward death = to go toward birth" means "the birth (of the book) = the death (of the author) = *the birth of the writer in the book*." We must not forget that this means giving birth to yourself in language. The death wish possesses a double: the desire to survive. Proustian death is theological: it postulates access to a "better world"—the imaginary, in opposition to the real. Thus we have the consecration of art in the *Recherche* generally, and in the madeleine scene itself, in the form of *religious* signifiers (madeleine-Madeleine, scallop shell—*coquille de Saint-Jacques*—religious folds) and signifieds (oral communion). The work of art is the epiphany of the self that has finally been found, the revelation of its ultimate singularity, the presence contained under the species of the book, resurrection beyond several deaths ("I already died many times since childhood"; II, 1116).

For Beckett, on the contrary, the author's death is the *death of the writer in the book*. Beneath "theories of literature," which are always rationalizations "after the fact," the original fantasy of fusion with the mother, the desire for non-difference, implies in Beckett the refusal of the subject who speaks *to distinguish himself* in language: "But it is useless to drag out this chapter of *my*, how shall I say, my existence, for it has no sense, to my mind" (*Molloy*, 56). Molloy, Moran: *my* (Mommy?). The primitive indistinction of existence deconstructs the Narrator's identity. To talk about yourself is to split yourself up into a multiplicity of tautological instances. The *deictic "I"* discovers its linguistic void in discourse. Both for the *here* and the *now*. From now on—without references—identity, spatiality, temporality are abolished in a new scriptural status: connotation without denotation. Word without object (no longer a word) and without origin (no longer a speaker), language is *anonymous*. Contrary to what is too quickly decided, this "anonymity" is not an observation; it is in no way "in the nature of language" as we speak of the "nature of things." It is the product of work: "For what I was doing neither for Molloy, who mattered nothing to me, nor for myself, of whom I despaired, but on behalf of a cause which, while having need of us to be accomplished, was in its essence anonymous, and would subsist, haunting the minds of men, when its miserable artisans should be no more" (*Molloy*, 114–15). In the early state of his undertaking, the Beckettian "scriptor" does not renounce all forms of the beyond, only those regarding his "work" from which he eliminates all personal traces. The "author's death," in Beckett, is not a natural death. It's a suicide.

Once again, it is by no means a matter of doing "literary history" or of "comparing" Proust and Beckett, but of following the path of fantasy in its logical articulations. I add that in any case the history of literature itself remains caught in imaginary structures; it is dependent upon a history not of literary "ideas" or "theories" but of the system of fantasies that governs them. From Horace's classical *"Exegi monumentum aere perennius"* to Baudelaire's "I give you these lines so that if my name should luckily reach distant times," the desire to escape death has been translated in the wish to immortalize the *name* of the subject of the words (the poet) or of their object (the person loved). Proust is situated in this ancient tradition, as we have seen. In and through his book he will offer himself identity and eternity, or at least a greater longevity than that of the flesh. To those he loves he will assure this "compensating glory," in the manner of Mlle Vinteuil's friend. Subjective doubts (ambivalence) or objective ones (culture's instability) within the Narrator leave intact the status of the literary work as *monument*, that is, as *tomb*; the Proustian variant, unlike that of Mallarmé, is the church cemetery, for which Saint Hilary's church at Combray offers the perfect metaphor.

Now since, to all appearances, we can find only words in the poetic tomb, the only remains of a being who endures should consist in his name alone. Yet a strange paradox remains. We have already commented upon the famous sentence: "A book is a great cemetery in which one can no longer decipher the half-effaced names on most of the graves" (II, 1018). But if the *names of others* are inscribed in their complete form (Albertine, grandmother, Gilberte, Mme de Guermantes) on any page, the only name which is "erased" is *that of the Narrator.* It is in fact "erased" from one end of the book to the other. Criticism has explicated at length the "anonymity" of the Proustian Narrator (to whom we have given a capital, since he is the only identity in the diverse instances subsumed under the "I" of the *Recherche*) without, however, really understanding his nature. We might well be surprised that in the "essentially anonymous" work that constitutes writing in Beckett, the speaker or scriptor should have a name: Molloy, Moran, Watt, Murphy, or another. If the verbal instance is namable, it's precisely because the name is *without importance.* Impersonal and empty, it has the value of a grammatical "connecting link." It is the place where language refers to its source, without any external reference; Molloy is Moran, as you and I are "I." The name's only signified is the play of the signifier to which it lends itself (*Sophie-sagesse* or Molloy-moly). Anonymity in Beckett means that no difference exists between personal pronoun and proper noun.

But this is not the case in Proust; we might even say that it's the exact opposite. In his study "Proust et les noms," Barthes has clearly demonstrated the metaphoric value of "phenomena of symbolic phoneticism" in Proust's writing ("orange light" in *Guermantes*, Stendhalian sweetness and the reflected love of violets in *Parme*, etc.); he concludes: "It is because the proper name lends itself to an infinitely rich catalysis that it is possible to say that, poetically speaking, the entire *Recherche* has emerged out of a few names."[21] Curiously enough, *only the proper name* possesses this catalytic or genetic quality for Proust—as the "etymological" obsessions of Combray's parish priest and of Brichot confirm. Rimbaud, on the contrary, will make his sonnet "emerge" from simple and democratic "vowels," while from Huysmans to Remy de Gourmont an "evocative enchantment" will be demanded of aristocratic, rare vocables—noble words, certainly, but common nouns.

My object here is not to explain this curious valorization of the proper noun, nor to wonder—if it is true, according to Barthes's remark, that for Proust as for Cratulus, "the virtue of nouns lies in teaching"—why this propaedeutic virtue is reserved to a single class. This is itself a separate study. We may perhaps take "class" in its political sense as well: someone who is noble is, precisely, someone who has "a name." It is the entire "history of France" that we get in the word *Guermantes*, as it is all that is common and Jewish in *Bloch*, or nouveau riche and precarious in *Swann*—snob and Dreyfusard—whose name is pronounced in two ways. Overestimating the name is an ideological choice in which Proust's "reactionary" side is showing. We might also, on another level, point out with Lévi-Strauss that proper names function in a special way for certain primitive societies that construct a sacred language in which they act as mediators: the Tiwi system, "if one defines it, on the most general level, as consisting in an exchange of words between the profane and the sacred language, through the medium of proper names" clarifies many of the phenomena that we find once again in our culture.[22] If, for Proust, literature is certainly a sacred language, or a sacred form of language, the Tiwi system is perhaps not so far from his system. As Lévi-Strauss also says, at the fringes of a general system of classification of which they are "both its extension and its limit," proper names are not without a connection to "some modes of classing, arbitrarily isolated under the title of totemism . . . among ourselves this 'totemism' has merely been humanized. Everything takes place as if in our civilization every individual's own personality were his totem: it is the signifier of his signified being" (p. 214).

What is noteworthy here is that the Narrator carefully disguises this "signifier" of his "being which is signified." While "his own personality" is the unique object of his discourse, he denies it all "totem." This attitude is all the more revealing in that at Combray, where it emerges, the hierarchy of beings is given in a nomenclature system. It's not because the name, as in Beckett, is without importance that the Proustian writer hides his own from us; it is because it is *essential*. We must point out that besides the mythopoeic function of the person's or country's name, the proper noun is the scene of an *erotic investment*. This investment is, of course, clearly ambivalent. Tinted with a historicizing phantasmagoria in the case of the Narrator's "feelings" for the Duchess of Guermantes, colored with romantic fables when "the name Gilberte passed close by me" (I, 301), the name quickly becomes the object of a strange fetishist cult:

I made every effort to introduce the name of Swann into my conversation with my parents; in my own mind, of course, I never ceased to murmur it; but I needed also to hear its exquisite sound, and to make myself play that chord, the voiceless rendering of which did not suffice me. . . . I analysed it, I spelt it; its orthography came to me as a surprise. And with its familiarity it had simultaneously lost its innocence. The pleasure that I derived from the sound of it I felt to be so guilty, that it seemed to me as though the others must read my thoughts. [I, 315]

We rediscover the rituals of adoration and profanation. Ceremoniously repeated or sadistically dismembered, the name is the substitute for the body. Thus beneath the surface guilt there exists a deeply rooted guilt attached to these false "innocent" games. With the name, the Narrator replays the same fantasies as with the person. Having just glimpsed Gilberte in the famous "hawthorn" scene, he concludes: "I loved her. I was sorry not to have had the time and the inspiration to insult her, to do her some injury" (I, 109). Receiving a letter from her, he subjects the signature of the one he loves to a strange graphic torture in which the destructive fantasy of a dismembered body is projected—understandably displaced, of course, on to Françoise: "Françoise declined to recognise Gilberte's name, because the elaborate capital 'G' leaning against the undotted 'i' looked more like an 'A,' while the final syllable was indefinitely prolonged by a waving flourish" (I, 383–84). Distortion of the "G" into an "A" (from Albertine, of course), castration of the "i," moving flourish that devours—the Narrator is the Blackbeard of Women's Names. Their cut-up cadavers combine, as the "telegram" scene in Venice attests, where Albertine's and Gilberte's *disjecta membra* cause the living woman's signature to be taken for that of the one who is dead: "The dot over the *i* of Gilberte had risen above the word to make the end of the message. As for her capital *G*, it resembled a gothic *A*"; also, "the tail of an *s* or *z* in the line above [had been read] as an '-ine' attached to the word 'Gilberte'" (II, 840). The Book, "cemetery" of words, is also a torture chamber of names.

Name and *first name* are, for better or for worse, in the ineluctable generality of signs, the index of a singular existence—even if, since it is multiple, this singularity proliferates in as many names and first names for a single character, such as Charlus, as are necessary to designate the diversity of his "selves." The Narrator is not a foundling; like everyone else, he possesses a family name and a first name. In fact, he makes several allusions to one and to the other: "She said to me 'You know, you may call me "Gilberte"; in any case, I'm going to call you by your first name.' . . . she . . . ended it with my Christian name" (I, 308). But the writer withholds from the reader these names that he reveals to the characters in the book. The *family name* is never mentioned. The *first name*, gradually "erased" in the course of successive editions, survives only in three brief references in *La Prisonnière*, which we will come back to. Of course, there is a paradoxical situation here which has caught the critics' attention and which Serge Gaubert summarizes very well: "It's a young man without a name who 'dreams about names.'"[23] Yet the Narrator's reticence is, in his system, normal. Since his relationship to the Other is fundamentally asymmetrical, he breaks off all reciprocity at the very point where it is formed—in the question, "What is your name? And you?" This real "taboo" concerning names has a specific cause, which we will of course seek in *Totem and Taboo:*

The strangeness of this taboo on names diminishes if we bear in mind that the savage looks upon his name as an essential part and an important possession of his personality. . . . civilized man . . . too is not yet as far removed as he thinks from attributing the importance of things to mere names and feeling that his name has been peculiarly identified with his person.[24]

The Proustian Narrator is not without resemblance to the patient Freud discusses:

One of these taboo patients, whom I knew, had adopted the avoidance of writing down her name for fear that it might get into somebody's hands who thus would come into possession of a piece of her personality. In her frenzied faithfulness, which she needed to protect herself against the temptations of her fantasy, she had created for herself the commandment, "not to give away anything of her personality." To this belonged first of all her name. [p. 76]

Such is, in fact, the Narrator's strategy. If, as we have seen, the Name is the substitute for the body, in regard to which the same conduct is repeated, we understand that with his name, the Narrator is hiding his face, his voice. It is the invisible man who watches Albertine sleep. Critics, notably Marcel Muller, have seen this: "Anonymity would, then, tend to sanction the Hero's preeminence over the other" (*Les Voix Narratives*, 17)—provided we add that here the Other is the *reader*. If we have defined reading as that Proustian trap to "catch the Other," the Narrator adequately disposes of empirical particularities so that through reading, *the Other becomes "I."*

His strategy is really the one Deleuze talks about: the strategy of the spider. The spider, is, of course, caught in his own web. From the instant that the Other becomes "I," *Je est un Autre*. In a flash, the success of writing turns into the failure of reading. The "unique accent," the "individuality" become alienated and are lost. If the very aim of the enterprise is to inscribe the *self* in a language, this *being with a proper name*, which is the Grail of the *Recherche*, is appropriated by the reader. The phantasmatic situation of writing previously defined—"I have being, so others don't have it"—reverses itself one more time to the benefit of the Other: "By reading me, he steals being from me." Thus he must avoid at all costs this "posthumous infidelity" to Albertine (II, 1018), whom each new reader steals from him in order to constitute his or her own substance. To assure this ipseity (won after a long and hard battle) in the nutritive circuit of reading, since the reader is not "edible," the only way remaining is to *make the Narrator unincorporable*. The only way to be unincorporable is to have *no body*. The only way to have no one take your identity is to be *unidentifiable*.

This is indeed the inflexible logic of fantasy that constructs the narrative instance, which sets in place the famous Proustian "I." The "being of flight" par excellence is Albertine only by projection; it is, of course, this Narrator, who has long been observed giving himself up in disguise to the other "characters," lending his *arrivisme* to Bloch and his taste for lucre to Morel, palming his homosexuality off onto Charlus. (I'm talking here about the Narrator, not about the signer of the book.) Supremely clever, is this distinction intentional or even possible? We are familiar with that pons asinorum of Proustian criticism in which opposing answers confront each other: *is the Narrator or is he not Marcel Proust?*— only to conclude generally that he is, without being he, while at the same time being he. We must be aware that the difficulty here is not ours; *it is on the part of the writer*. It is at this point, I think, that the systems of fantasy and of writing, which have been united until now, burst open and separate, leaving a gap that cannot be filled.

◀ 10 ▶

Here we are, then (it's really Proustian), suddenly sent back to the beginning, to the initial question: if the madeleine scene functions as a screen-memory, what does the Narrator hide from *us* and from *himself*? If he hides his name from us, what does he hide from himself by hiding it from us? We saw that in withholding his name from us, he wants to withhold his person, and for what reason, by what strategy. But what does he withhold from himself, or what is withheld from him? And precisely what in the experience or, rather, in the writing of the scene? "She sent out for one of those short, plump little cakes called 'petites madeleines,' which look as though they had been moulded in the fluted scallop of a pilgrim's shell" (1, 34).

Two remarks command our attention, following the order of the signifiers. (1) Capital letters are certainly unjustified for cakes that we are told are among the most ordinary;[25] they are later abandoned—"the sight of the little madeleine," (1, 36), etc.—constituting in this way a graphic hapax. (2) We find, in a kind of "mirror image" at the end of the sentence, the scallop shells (*coquilles de Saint-Jacques*) in which the "Petites Madeleines" are, so to speak, typographically "moulded." Now, if *"coquilles de Saint-Jacques"* is a common noun formed with a proper noun (underlined by the use of *de* in the expression), *Petites Madeleines* appears as a proper noun formed with a common one (it serves precisely to "name": *"called Petites Madeleines"*). Hence the capitals, which are also initials in which the name is made legible: *P*etites *M*adeleines = *P*(roust) *M*(arcel). The taboo clearly functions in both senses: prohibition (censorship) and consecration (by metonymy, *Saint-Jacques*). Thus, what is ultimately repressed in the madeleine scene, which naturally leaves its trace, is the *Narrator's name*. He not only hides his *identity* from others but rejects it for himself; he wants to be *unidentifiable* for himself. The Proustian "I" refuses to be called "Marcel Proust."

Of course, criticism has long interpreted this "refusal" *in an exterior way* as a conscious choice, even a technique of the novelist. A man named Marcel Proust decides to use his real self as the analogon for a fictive "I." The problem, then, would be more or less to gauge the degree to which the real Proust flows into the imaginary Narrator. This is to miss, I think, the essence of the problem and the meaning of the *Recherche*. The man-named-Marcel-Proust *cannot* be the Proustian "I," not because such and such biographical detail is changed or omitted but *in principle:* "It is not a question of knowing whether I speak of myself in a way that conforms to what I am, but rather of knowing whether I am the same as that of which I speak" (*Ecrits*, 165). That the subject is "split open" by his discourse, that an absolute cleavage separates for him the order of Being and the order of the Logos is neither Freud's "discovery" nor Lacan's, but Proust's; his whole book consists in the setting in place of the transparent and unbridgeable distance that divides "I" as referent from "I" as reference, subject of existence ("hero") from subject of discourse ("Narrator"). It's a question here not of a temporal disjunction but of an ontological break. The madeleine experience is crucial. It abolishes the temporal disjunction between present "sensation" and past "sensation"; existential fragments of the subject coincide. Now, at the moment when he experiences, in the form of continuity, his *identity in being* ("all this long stretch of time . . . was . . . my very self"; II, 1123), he refuses his identity in language by repressing his name, proclaiming a radical discontinuity between the real and the symbolic.

Fantasy says, *I want to be me.* The text says, *my name is not me.* The place of the madeleine is the scene of a tragic conflict: to be yourself, you have to abandon your name. If the Narrator proves to be sensitive to the fact that "our social personality is created by the thoughts of other people" (I, 15), with better reason our nominal identity constitutes complete alienation. We possess it only because of the Other. It is understandable that the madeleine experience, which is one of ipseity, rejects this Otherness.

A minimal trace, which is a minimal identification, remains of the repression in the form of *initials.* These initials are presented in a certain *order* which it is appropriate to question: P.M.—Proust comes before Marcel here. Family name and first name: this is the order of civil status, establishing the precedence of the patronymic. Looking more closely at the graphism, we see that it is the place where a strange insistence of the letter *P* occurs—for Proust, but also for *Père* (father); *M* for Marcel, but also for Mother. This is symbolism that the text later confirms; the only time the Narrator's first name "escapes," it's from the lips of Mamma-Albertine: *in bed* (II, 429); a second (and last) mention of it is written—also by the same female hand (II, 488). Bed, birth: you are (born) *Marcel.* But you are *Proust.* The name-of-the-father remains the only legitimate insertion in symbolic organization for the subject in the society he lives in. In the Narrator's case, things became complicated; *he cannot be Proust. He cannot identify* with the identifying instance. The real father—at once slow-witted and colorless, debonair and weak, a Sunday "weatherman" who "always manages to get his bearings" during the walks—represents what his son hates most: the "principle of reality" or, to be more exact, of "realism." He must constantly look somewhere else for his "ideal self," in the open-ended series of imaginary paternal identifications: Swann at first, of course, but also Bergotte and Elstir, not to speak of the equivocal relationship with Charlus, whose homosexuality willingly takes on paternalistic traits.

Now despite their obvious differences, all these imaginary fathers have one point in common. As Saint Peter possesses the keys to heaven, they control access to the world of Art, forbidden to the real father: speech (Swann, Charlus); writing (Bergotte); painting (Elstir); music (let's not forget an "unhappy father," Vinteuil). In the creation of languages, men produce; women consume. A future writer therefore needs a *masculine model.* We can easily see the consequences for the Narrator. Reading Bergotte, he tells us, "I wept upon his printed page, as in the arms of a long-lost father" (I, 73). Bergotte is the father who was lacking. But a father he adopts is never the real father who alone can give the son his *name.* This should be taken literally: as a *writer,* the Narrator *has no father. His name cannot be Proust.* As a writer, we have seen, all his primary identifications are with the maternal imago (Mamma, grandmother, Aunt Léonie). The only name the Narrator of the *Recherche* can bear is his first name: *Marcel.*

Between *Marcel* and *Proust* there is a civil war going on, a kind of intestinal struggle. At the moment during the madeleine scene when present sensation and past sensation fuse in the identity of an existence, the Narrator cannot make it coincide with the *identity* of a proper name. Family names and first names are juxtaposed without being united. A gap that cannot be filled separates them. Each stays, so to speak, on its own side, each on its own "way"; *the two ways*, of course, are those projected into the "walks" at Combray, with which the Narrator, without ever being able to unite them, alternately identifies his childhood quest: "For there were, in the environs of Combray, two 'ways' which we used to take for four walks, and so diametrically opposed that we would actually leave the house by a different door, according to the way we had chosen: the way towards Méséglise-la-Vineuse, which we called also 'Swann's way' . . . and the 'Guermantes way'" (I, 103).

"*Swann's way*": the way where you find the imaginary father, of course, par excellence, whom he gives to himself in his "familial novel" (he will write this novel, *Swann in Love*), but also the way where the real father is first found, doubled if need be by the grandfather, with whom the child undertakes the Great Walk to Tansonville (I, 104). It is the way of adolescent virile identifications, the *aubépines* (hawthorne)—*aube* (dawn) and *pine*—awakening erotic desire, which causes to emerge in succession (1) "out of a straw basket lying forgotten on the grass by the side of a line" (I, 105), at the end of a curious descriptive syntagma (stocks opening "their fresh plump purses," "on the gravel-path a long watering-pipe, painted green," the "prismatic fan" of its "drops"), a "little girl, with fair reddish hair"—*Gilberte* (I, 108); (2) the imaginary *Roussainville peasant girl*, upon whom the child "crystallizes" (I, 120); (3) *Mlle Vinteuil* (I, 122) and the scene of "sadism"—that is, the series of real, fictive, and substitutive objects of the sex drive.

The *Guermantes way*: the way of the ideal mother, thus a way that is inaccessible ("Nor could we ever reach that other goal, to which I had longed so much to attain, Guermantes itself"; I, 131); the way where identification is *feminine*, desired but forbidden; river landscape, the "walks along the 'Guermantes way'" consist in a vain and significant effort to penetrate as far as the source of the Vivonne (I, 131). In the absence of the source of life, you penetrate as far as the sources of language, to the resources of poetic procreation, which revolve around the revery of the name, "bathed, as in a sunset, in the orange light which glowed from the resounding syllable 'antes'" (I, 132). Of all the functions of female identification, the essential one clearly appears. The Guermantes way is the way where you find the *desire to write*. "Since I wished, some day, to become a writer, it was high time to decide what sort of books I was going to write" (I, 132). To the question posed here, to which the answer is naively asked of the *father* ("Perhaps this want of talent . . . would be brought to an end by the intervention of my father"; I, 133), the answer will be provided at the end of the book, at the *Guermantes* party. The desire for an ideal maternity (which is permitted) in language, which forms the basis for the desire to write, gives birth in this very spot to the *first text* of the future author: the description of the Martinville bell towers (I, 139). In addition, like the presence of the real father along "Swann's way," the presence of the real mother along the "Guermantes way" is visible: in the fantasy which, curiously, makes of "Geneviève de Brabant"—maternal projection of the "magic lantern"—an "ancestress of the Guermantes family" (I, 132); in the memory, taken from the same unconscious chain, of the bedtime scene and of "my mother's face" (I, 140), which suddenly emerges at the right moment and ends the description of the second "way."

If our analysis is exact; if, for the Narrator, masculine identity is identification with the father's name (Proust), omitted *from* the book but present *on* the book—the printed signature is a *textual* element—and reappearing in the return of the repressed ("Petites Madeleines"); if, in addition, his female identity is identification with the mother's-first-name (Marcel), then the distance that separates his *family* and *first* names is the same as that which divides the *two ways* of Combray: "I set between them, far more distinctly than the mere distance in miles and yards and inches which separated one from the other, the distance that there was between the two parts of my brain in which I used to think of them" (I, 103). This disposition or, rather, this schizoid position explains many of the Narrator's disappointments ("the Méséglise and Guermantes 'ways' left me exposed, in later life, to much disillusionment, and even to many mistakes"; I, 142), if it is true—as Freud says in the passage on the proper noun already quoted—that obsessional neurotics "derive a good many, often serious, inhibitions from their treatment of their own name" (*Totem and Taboo*, 76). *Proust-Marcel* (parallel to the order of the syntagma: *Swann-Guermantes*), *male-female*—the nominal being of the Narrator is *androgynous*. We might say that the "first appearance of the men-women" talked about in *Sodom and Gomorrah* (II, 3) under the cover of repression occurs *there*: at the place of the madeleine, of the *Petites Madeleines*. Carefully purged from the Narrator's apparent desires, projected in a kind of systematic delirium upon the other characters in the *Recherche*, the homosexual obsession is inscribed in the bisexual condition "of which certain rudiments of male organs in the anatomy of the woman, and of female organs in that of the man seem still to preserve the trace" (II, 24). "That initial hermaphroditism" is given here as a kind of *hermaphroditism* of *initials*.

Deleuze has clearly understood the meaning of this: "Hermaphroditism is not the property of a now-lost animal totality, but the actual partitioning of the two sexes in one and the same plant: 'the male organ is separated by a partition from the female organ' [II, 22]."[26] If, for the sex theorist that the Narrator is, "transsexualism" sets in place a complex relational system—a kind of combinative machine for objects, remarkably well analyzed by Deleuze, "in which a man also seeks what is masculine in a woman, and a woman what is feminine in a man, and this in the partitioned contiguity of the two sexes as partial objects" (p. 121)—the fertilization process implies a break in partitioning by means of a kind of *transversal communication*. Proust's sexologist views, however, pose a particular problem for the writer.

The book's creation, in fact, is modeled upon procreation: the metaphor of the book-child and its conception, which induces pregnancy symptoms. The *Temps retrouvé* opens and closes precisely with the "departitioning of the two ways," without which fertilization is impossible (here the sexual meaning of the "two ways" at Combray becomes obvious). In the first pages, Gilberte's remark—"If you like, we could just as well go out one afternoon, and go to Guermantes, by way of Méséglise, that's the nicest way" substitutes continuity for contiguity. The "two ways," which the Narrator thought separate, actually meet. In the final pages, Mlle de Saint-Loup's presence, a starlike crossroads where various paths converge, suddenly causes to "come to an end in her the two principal 'ways' where I had taken so many walks, and dreamed so many dreams" (ii, 1110). Swann's granddaughter in this way becomes the metaphor or the emblem of the fundamental convergence that constitutes the book (itself woven around and beginning with Swann; ii, 1027), the conjunction of the paternal and maternal "ways" in the child-book.

This "conjunction" is not the attribute of heterosexual relations. Used to designate the meeting between Charlus and Jupien (ii, 26), the word reminds us that the apparent diversity of the metaphorical systems by means of which the Narrator describes homosexual behavior (botanical and entomological: flower-insect, bee-orchid, etc.) also assumes an act of fertilization:

Like so many creatures of the animal and vegetable kingdom, like the plant which would produce vanilla, but because in its structure the male organ is divided by a partition from the female, remains sterile unless the humming birds or certain tiny bees convey the pollen from one to the other, or man fertilises them by artificial means, M. de Charlus (and here the word fertilise must be understood in a moral sense, since in the physical sense the union of male with male is and must be sterile . . .) was one of those men who may be called exceptional. [ii, 22]

Physical or moral, Proustian fertilization consists of a process in which the barrier that separates male from female in a single individual is surmounted (penetrated, skirted) through the intermediary of an outside agent: that is, through the mediation of the Other. You will remember the Narrator's three abortive knocks on the "partition" that separates him from his grandmother at Balbec, which is grounded in the same fantasy. Identity and fertilization are moments of the same process (or of the same fantasy): the *Recherche* for the self that is absolute, for the essence that is unique. If, as we have shown, the writer's desire is to become his own mother, to give birth to himself in language, we are not surprised that the dream of artistic autogenesis is *consciously* offered in the metaphor of biological parthenogenesis, that the writer clings to this metaphor and is fascinated by it:

An exceptional act of autofecundation *comes at a given point to apply its turn of the screw, its pull on the curb, brings back within normal limits the flower that has exaggerated its transgression of them. My reflexions had followed a tendency which I shall describe in due course, and I had already drawn from the visible stratagems of flowers a conclusion that bore upon a* whole unconscious element of literary work. [II, 4–5]

From artistic *self-contemplation* (II, 490) to creative *autofecundation:* such is, so to speak, the itinerary or program of the *Recherche.*

Self-fecundation, we notice, is presented as a "turn of the screw," a "pull on the curb," a *restriction* imposed by nature on the proliferation that occurs through cross-breeding (II, 4). If the "ruse of the flowers" is apparent, what is the *ruse of art,* whose importance for "a whole unconscious element of literary work" has been mentioned to us? Literature, like all cultural works, is grounded in the structure of the Oedipal complex. The writer's relationship to the repressed name *Proust Marcel* is inscribed in the triangle father-mother-son. Writing is the mythic resolution of the Oedipal complex: the son kills the father (omits his name), by means of a "restriction" that functions in the symbolic order as the homologue of that which functions in the natural order. *Marcel* is total identification with the *Mother,* incorporated (eaten) mother; in the madeleine, incest is literally "consummated." It can be read, just as literally, in the choice of *François le Champi* to close the Combray bedtime scene and to open the final meditation at the Guermantes matinée: "the story of a foundling who is loving and sensitive, who is mothered by a young woman who runs a mill. He feels a deep attachment for her, an exclusive tenderness which becomes, with age, the love of a man for a woman. He will in the end marry his adoptive mother."[27] The father is dead, the mother is married; the results of the Oedipal operation are given to the *letter*.

From the proper noun, only the *M* of Mother and of Marcel, and also the *M* of Me, survives. The act of "autofecundation," the "ruse of art," is to conclude: *Me is I*. The "partition" separating the male and female parts is abolished. The "conjunction" of the "two ways," necessary even for homosexual fertilization, is assured. "I" is finally, for the Narrator, the ultimate *essence* of the identity he seeks; the precise *form* of this "transversal communication" with himself (symbolized at the end of the book in the simultaneous epiphany of Mlle de Saint-Loup and the writer); the warp to reweave the continuous into the weft of the discontinuous; the "intersection" or "crossroads" of all the "selves" that have dispersed or disappeared: "There must have been no break of continuity, not a moment of rest for me, no cessation of existence, of thought, of consciousness of myself, since this distant moment still clung to me and I could recapture it, merely by descending more deeply within myself" (II, 1123). I would say without hesitation that the final fulfillment of the nutritional fantasy in the Proustian writer is *grammatical digestion: the mother is assimilated into Me and becomes I*.

A text of Jakobson on the child's relationship to the use of the personal pronoun allows us to articulate an analysis that is both linguistic and psychoanalytic:

He can hesitate to speak of himself in the first person whereas his interlocutors call him "you." Sometimes he tries to redistribute these appellations. . . . Finally, "I" can be so rigorously substituted by the child for his own name that he comes to name immediately the people in his entourage, but obstinately refuses to pronounce his own name. For its young bearer, then, the name has only a vocative signification, opposed to the nominative function of the "I." This attitude can survive as a vestige from childhood.[28]

Such is the case of the Narrator, whose own name, which he refuses to state, has a vocative value. Gilberte calls him by his "Christian name" (I, 308), which will be given by Albertine; his "name" is the object of an aggressive impertinence and associated, as Muller has noticed, with a "danger": distorted by the Italian employers

(II, 833); shouted by the Guermantes flunkies (II, 30); whispered by mocking servants (II, 1037). Coming from others, used by others, your own name is the symbol of being-for-others. It is understandable that the Narrator, searching for his singularity, refuses this "totemic" possession. But it is more than that. In the text quoted, Jakobson mentions the example of another writer: "In this way Guy de Maupassant admitted that his name, when he pronounced it himself, sounded extremely strange to his ears."

That the subject *has* a name but *is* not that name explains this "strangeness." Benveniste's remarks clarify this: "*Etre* establishes an intrinsic relationship of equivalence between the two terms it joins: it is the consubstantial state. In contrast the two terms joined by *avoir* remain distinct; the relationship between them is extrinsic and could be called 'pertinential'; it is the relationship of the possessed to the possessor."[29] The "intrinsic relationship of equivalence," offered in Proustian experience at the level of existence by the instantaneous fusion of past and present, cannot be obtained at the level of language by identification with a name. The only linguistic entity that you can *be* is neither a family name nor any proper noun but a *pronoun*. A name is a pseudo-identity; assumed to "suit a single person," it may always have homonyms. It is an occasion for constant ambiguity.[30] This is the problem of Giraudoux's *Amphitryon*, the "true Amphitryon" not necessarily being "the Amphitryon where you dine." In fact, as elements of a classification system, to the extent that family and first names share in the status of the proper noun—despite their individual nature—they belong to the domain of the "third person"; that is, according to Benveniste, they escape the "condition of person." The only form of being present to yourself, the unique linguistic index of identity, is "I": "*I* signifies the person who is uttering the present instance of the discourse containing *I*" (*PGL*, 281).

"For a long time I used to go to bed early." The first sentence of the *Recherche* is also the final discovery. Without giving the details here of an analysis that appears elsewhere, I would point out that the *Je me* of *Je me suis couché de bonne heure* makes the subject and object of the reflexive verb coincide. The one who *no longer* goes to bed early (and who alone can grammatically state this sentence) is *the same person* as the one who for a long time went to bed early. Here we have a kind of *linguistic equivalence of the madeleine scene*, expression and remembrance functioning *en abîme*, one the metaphor for the other. The substitution of *je me* for Proust Marcel liberates the very possibility of the *Recherche*.

The narrative, epistemological, and even ethical consequences of this "choice" have for a long time been well analyzed; we have long been aware that everything in the *Recherche* revolves around the complex play of the "I." In the context of this essay it is important to demonstrate the curious operation of what could be called a "phantasmatic grammar." Different from the "he" or "she" of the classic *récit* in which the narrative introduces the difference of the sexes, and different from the first name *Marcel* in which the legible identification is masculine, the bisexual "I" gives the Narrator the means to resolve his fantasies. Swann's way and the Guermantes way meet *linguistically;* the barrier separating male and female parts falls; autofecundation becomes possible. Analogous to the insect and the orchid, "I" reunites the divided hermaphrodite with "himself." But in opposition to what happens in the natural order, the fertilizing agent is not a *third* party; it is *the same person. I =* Proust-Marcel = *Père-Mère*. Since, according to Lévi-Strauss, the Oedipal myth is "a kind of logical tool which relates the original problem—born from one or born from two?—to the derivative problem: born from different or born from same?"[31] we could say that the Narrator's grammatical fantasy is presented as a singularly regressive version. To the Sphinx's question, which the seductive and devouring figure of the mother sets forth in the Champs-Elysées restroom, the Narrator answers, *I am born of I, who is the same as the other.* In the *literalness* of this fantasy of autofecundation, *I* erases *P and assimilates the still visible M* of Mother and of Me.

The parthenogenesis the writer dreams about does not abolish the sexes in the least; it mixes them. More precisely, what it suppresses is their difference. By *being* "I," since this personal pronoun—unlike family and first names—escapes the distinction of gender, the Narrator situates his person in sexual indistinction. We see him in turn "son" to Mamma; "brother," "son," and "mother" to Albertine (II, 456, 459), and her "lover," too; equally, "mother" of his book; mockingly, for the servants, "the father" (II, 1037). The rigid separation of the two "ways" at Combray is replaced by a strange fluidity in which the permutation of roles espouses and exhausts sexual possibilities. The "autofecundated" writer is the Proteus of chromosomes. If we have been able to say that at a final level Combraysian fantasy is nostalgia for a before-birth paradise, "I" possesses embryonic sex—*both of them*, according to the science of the period. Linguistic fantasy joins up once again with intrauterine fantasy in an identical reversal of signs. Just as if time "beyond time" were that of "before time," "I" is the only name you can have before the name, since you are named only at birth. Suddenly at this point Proust already joins Beckett: the writer is a *talking fetus*.

The series that the imagination creates do not appear at random. The grammar of fantasy possesses strict rules. The *récit's* generativity, which sets in motion the narrative possibilities of the subject who says "I," is inscribed in the same problematic as the generation of any *narrator*. If, as linguists tell us, the referent "I" and the reference "I" are distinct, we may ask of the *récit*, "Born of one, or born of two?" "Born of the same, or of the other?" From whichever angle we approach it, the problem of the *subject* remains grounded in the structure of the Oedipal myth. The question of being (who am I?) is necessarily qualified by the question of sex (I am of what sex?). The Proustian Narrator has understood this so well that in his quest for identity he has become not only a *psychologist* but also a *sexologist*. Hence the great "theory of sex" with which he provides himself en route and which we have encountered. But as we already said in regard to "reasoning," in Proust "theory" serves fantasy—of which it is an additional manifestation—for purposes of self-justification. Beyond what it says, it means, "The sex of the Other is not important, since *I* have all of them."

We can easily guess what it was in Proust that seduced Deleuze: what there is of man in a woman and of woman in a man, seeking what there is of woman in a man and of man in a woman—the

Proustian system of "partial objects" prefigures Deleuze's "desiring machines." But this is to misunderstand that in Proust the system is *pure fantasy*, and the proof is that the Narrator's own "theory" does not reassure him in the least. Whereas Deleuze tells us that by virtue of Proustian logic alone, it is absurd to wonder, as some have done, whether Albertine is a disguised Albert—contrary to this so-called logic, that is exactly the question which the Narrator continues to ask himself, from which he continues to suffer, which is his torture beyond death: what is the nature of Albertine's *true* sexuality? Whereas his "transsexual" theory should offer him a universal model for comprehension, what particularly torments the Narrator is that despite his efforts (which go as far as having two laundresses make love in a brothel; Pléiade III, 550), he cannot imagine the quality of pleasure that a woman can have with a woman. Jealousy demystifies the theory of sexual undifferentiation. Despite the fact that it is entirely made up of partial drives, *sensual pleasure* is accessible only within the structure of global sex.

We are not surprised that at the end of this study of the central fantasy in the *Recherche*, the diverging series that we discovered can be flawlessly articulated: they order the question of being around the question of sex, of the being of sexuality. No personal identity without sexual identification. After the exhaustion of fantasy in the machine that combines the impossible, we find what we had in the beginning: *anxiety*—that of Oedipus confronting the Sphinx, that of the child confronting Oedipus.

The symbolic path that goes from Combray I to Combray II, crossing the madeleine scene, does indeed situate the moment of the work's creation—the point of departure for the *Recherche* as such—in the Oedipal structure, but does so in order to reverse systematically all kinds of normal resolution. We go from a *negative Oedipus* (Combray I: identification with the mother) to a *negation of Oedipus* (Combray II: autofecundation of "I") through the intermediary of an *imaginary liquidation* (madeleine: name-of-the-father eliminated, mother incorporated). Here we find Guy Rosolato's "fantasy of having fulfilled the fantasy," which "possesses the special quality of being situated in the unconscious as a memory." According to the same author, this is a well-known trait of the obsessional neurotic: "What strikes us is the neurotic's original way of avoiding castration and, consequently, the resolution of the Oedipal complex. He in fact constructs his Oedipal fantasy *as if it had already taken shape*: the Father killed, the Mother possessed. Given this, castration no longer needs to be considered; only guilt persists; that is why it can be so strong in him."[32]

It is obvious that the Narrator's constant questioning of the sex of the Other (is he or is he not homosexual? or bisexual? What position does he occupy in the combining machine of sex?) is an anguished projection of the questioning of *his own sex*. The Narrator's anonymity is very convenient here. Invisible, he possesses the sex of angels. In his capacity as citizen he is male. Not wanting to undertake here a study of the Narrator's sexuality—or rather, asexuality—we can say that he strolls through the *Recherche* like the "poet" whom he notices in one of Elstir's paintings: "Here and there a poet, of a race that had also a peculiar interest for the zoologist (characterised by a certain sexlessness) strolled with a Muse, as one sees in nature creatures of different but of kindred species consort together" (I, 1019). The poet has this in common with the Muse: he flees carnal relations. Whereas the other characters are obsessed by Eros, the Narrator displays a curious abstinence. He loves mature women, at a distance; little girls, chastely; at most, he masturbates on Albertine. His sexual "exploits," with good reason, are never described to us. Whether he is with the young cousin on the sofa or the servant at Doncières, he screws backstage, in retrospective accounts—never, so to speak, on stage. His "virility," duly confirmed, remains *allusive*.

He does not, however, hide his face so completely that we do not catch a glimpse of it: he is "too beautiful for a boy" (I, 315). We understand why the woman in pink exclaims: "How he resembles his mother" (I, 58). The boy-girl must, however, confront the rite of passage from sexual ambiguity to official masculinity, the symbolic approach of castration in the form of the cutting of his "curls": "While I was asleep I had returned without the least effort to an earlier stage in my life, now forever outgrown; and had come under the thrall of one of my childish terrors, such as that old terror of my great-uncle's pulling my curls, which was effectively dispelled on the day—the dawn of a new era to me—on which they were finally cropped from my head" (I, 4). Although it is presented in a positive way, the event is *important* enough to constitute a traumatism, often relived in dreams, in which the primitive terror is the object of an obvious displacement. The desire to "remain a girl," thwarted by the father (in the form of his "great-uncle's" cruelty), appears very clearly in the remarkable passage in which the Narrator describes Albertine's nudity:

Before Albertine obeyed and allowed me to take off her shoes, I opened her chemise. Her two little upstanding breasts were so round that they seemed not so much to be an integral part of her body as to have ripened there like fruit; and her belly (concealing the place where a man's is marred as though by an iron clamp left sticking in a statue that has been taken down from its niche) was closed, at the junction of her thighs, by two valves of a curve as hushed, as reposeful, as cloistral as that of the horizon after the sun has set. [II, 432]

This extraordinary text, rich in symbolic associations, commands attention—except, apparently, that of criticism, which has hardly commented upon it. We will make only a few remarks within the scope of our analysis. *Breast and vagina:* Albertine's nudity is *the madeleine.* The "round" breasts, which appear to grow on the body like "fruit" rather than to constitute an "integral part" of it, form the puffed side of the cake. From "fluted scallop of a pilgrim's shell," "valves of a curve," we recognize the other side. In both cases femininity is the object of desire, implicit in the madeleine scene, now completely explicit: desire not *to have* woman, but *to be* woman. This reversal of the virile position of desire is here tied specifically to the *phallic object* out of which all identification, masculine or feminine, is articulated; it is a direct confession unique in the entire *Recherche.* The radical depreciation of the phallus, at first disguised by aesthetic considerations ("the place where a man's is marred"), derives from the ontological priority attributed to woman. "Clamp left sticking in": the penis is an organ that is *residual* relative to an original integrity ("statue that has been taken down from its niche"). The personal myth of the Proustian neurotic is *just the opposite* of the official myth—which he calls to his rescue in the following paragraph to reestablish the traditional hierarchy: "O mighty attitudes of Man and Woman, in which . . . Eve is astonished and submissive before the Man by whose side she has awoken, as he himself, alone still, before God Who has fashioned him" (II, 433). Strange bombast, a very suspect religiosity, summoned in time to mask the too strident desire to be Woman. The "curve" of the identification follows exactly that of Albertine's "two valves": "sleepy," "reposing," "confining." *Hushed, reposeful, cloistral:* the Narrator's fantasy takes on Aunt Léonie's sex. "The horizon after the sun has set," literally that of his aunt after Uncle Octave has died.

If it is indeed true that the sun is "a sublimated symbol of the Father,"[33] then we must correct what we said in the interpretation of the masturbation scene in *Contre Sainte-Beuve:* "Wishing to sit down without being incommoded by the sun which was shining full on the seat, I quoted to it: 'Take yourself off, my boy, to make room for me'" (CSB, 31). It is more complex than evacuation (since we are in the "water-closet") of the female imago, masturbation in the form of a negation of the mother. In wanting to take his place in the "sun," the child wants *to put himself in his Father's place.* As an affirmation of omnipotence ("all this world reposed on me"), the rejection of the "swelling hillsides" ("mere insubstantial reflections") seeks *masculine affirmation* in the masturbatory act. "Take yourself off, my boy, to make room for me"; it is a happy episode of incest.

But the child cannot put himself in his father's place, because he is in his mother's. *Her belly concealing the place where a man's is marred as though by an iron clamp:* such is clearly the truth of the Proustian phallus. You cling to your "clamp" as well as you can, which is not very well at all, in a delusive show of virility, your official identity. The Narrator will go to Doncières to see others do their military service. Out of a sense of duty, he is a man. But the "statue which has been taken down from its niche" needs to recover its original, primary half. *Her belly (concealing the place):* secret desire for disguise, for suppression of the bothersome organ ("clamp"), promoter of a fictional identity. The *place of the madeleine* is the belly finally rid of the penis that clings to it, *finally castrated.*

The description of Albertine's sex can be superimposed with precision upon the madeleine scene; it presents a posteriori the condition for the possibility of that scene: the desire for feminization implies the desire for castration. But at this point we have to rectify our earlier construction, which superimposed the madeleine scene and the masturbation scene too rigorously. The two scenes are clearly homologous but not analogous. They are grounded in the same affective configuration: omnipotence, freedom from death, pleasure in the self. But the pleasure is not of the same sex in the two scenes. In masturbation the penis is the instrument in an exalting and ecstatic pleasure even in the face of the threat of castration ("agitated," "terrified," as if facing a "surgical operation"; CSB, 30). In the period when the Oedipal complex revives ("when I was twelve years old"; CSB, 30), the young boy tries to identify with the father and struggles to reject the maternal imago. The madeleine scene, which cannot be localized with any rigor but which is very late (the Narrator is an adult), presents itself as a recognition of the failure of the normal Oedipal resolution. From "Mamma" to "Aunt Léonie," from "Aunt Léonie" to the "ideal maternity" that is the book, the series of identifications is strictly feminine. Contrary to what occurs in the *Contre Sainte-Beuve,* where virile, genital pleasure offers the Narrator the identity he seeks ("individuality" of the jet of water/orgasm), in the episodes of the madeleine and of Albertine's sex, the penis is transformed into an *obstacle* to the identification he desires. To be "like his Mother," that is, to become "the Mother of his book," the Narrator fantasizes the loss of his penis.

In a more general way, if the phallus is the signifier of the fundamental difference between the sexes, its presence is an impediment to the formation of the system of symbiosis of which we have tried to show the symbolic concatenation in the *Recherche*: fusion of mother and son; absorption of the one he loves by the lover; coincidence of past and present; interpenetration of writer and reader; union of metaphoric opposites; dissolution of words in the substance of style. The Proustian dream of ultimate non-difference operates at all levels: "There must have been no break of continuity" (II, 1123). The price of continuity is phallic castration. It remains the task of the writer—and it is in this way that he imposes his authority—to take on the castration, which is desired, feared, rejected in the traditional "fantasy of having fulfilled the fantasy," avoided by all of the hero's subterfuges which try in turn to reverse, neutralize, or deny the presence of Oedipus.

Proustian fantasy says, *I want to be me.* The madeleine text says, *my name is not me.* The Narrator says, *me is I.* You must accept the consequence: I am unnamable. As we said earlier: no personal identity that is not sexual identity. Autofecundation of I, who is born of the same; pure polymorphous transsexuality; Proteus's sex or the embryo's—we have attempted to follow the multiple networks of fantasy that lure the desire of the writer. But any effort, as in this case, to escape the Oedipal myth constitutes a myth that presupposes it; the Oedipal myth remains fundamental. Partial drives or partial sexual objects, the discontinuities of a shifting Eros are always restructured within the triangle. Oedipus is the anti-Deleuze—and the anti-Proust. Father already killed, Mother already possessed: the confrontation with castration is useless to the Narrator, all the more so because his ultimate desire is not to love his Mother but to be her. If the encounter with castration is the equivalent of a separation from the mother, we understand why he has to avoid it at all costs. "*I*," in short, plays the game of his double sex: going the way of *P* (Proust-*Père*), he resolves the classical Oedipal complex in fantasy; going the way of *M* (Marcel-*Mère*), he enjoys his imaginary femininity in peace. But this is only to forget that female identity also confronts castration. The writer gives himself the penis he *wants* to be without by means of a symbolic exchange which imitates that of the woman, in the form of the *work-child*. But at the moment when he gives himself the "child," he takes it away; while he thinks he is immortalizing himself in it, he is cutting himself off from it. With a strange kind of revenge, the suppressed *Père* returns the mutilation of which he is a victim. Elision of *P*, the symbolic castration of the father, becomes—to the extent that he wants to be a writer—the *actual castration of the son*. Such is the price of the Narrator's imaginary maternity, or, if you wish, such is the ransom he pays for the sex of his writing.

In a patrilineal society, the rejection of the patronymic is not without its consequences. The Narrator does not liquidate his "totem" with impunity. If the *Recherche* is the narration of a literary "vocation" (ii, 1016), its formula is not simply "I wished, some day, to become a writer" (i, 133). The desire soon becomes specific—curiously enough, by invoking the power of the father: "Perhaps this want of talent . . . would be brought to an end by the intervention of my father, who would arrange with the Government and with Providence that I should be the first writer of my day" (i, 133). Father-Government-Providence: the desire to write is linked to the desire for official recognition. This means not "being a writer" but being "the first writer of my day." The denial of the irony nevertheless reveals a deep-seated wish. The Proustian writer is a hermit only out of professional need; the life of a recluse is a methodological necessity (sleep during the day, work at night). The desire of the writer, like that of the snob, intersects with desire for the Other; he thinks of himself situated in a hierarchy—like the snob once again—only "at the top." A writer, yes, but *famous*.

This notoriety is, moreover, necessary to assure those you love that "immortal and compensating glory" which Mlle Vinteuil and her friend gave to the dead musician. To save from oblivion is, as we have seen, the sacred function of art. While the laws of death and language mean the dissolution of his being, the artist subverts these laws; at the point where others are lost, he finds his irreducible "difference," affirms his most intimate "individuality." From this point of view, we have said that the motto of the *Recherche* could be "Others die so that I may return from the dead." The need for immortality, for himself and for others, is of course tempered by resignation in the face of the inevitable: life will undoubtedly die out on earth; perhaps the work will last only a hundred years, or ten. Waiting for the absolute reign of Nothingness, the Narrator re-writes untiringly on the tombs of his book-cemetery names that are erased: Albertine, grandmother, Gilberte, Mme de Guermantes—every name, in fact, *except his own*. Earlier in our interpretation we underlined the strategic advantages of this operation. It remains for us to assess the final cost.

We might say that the meaning of the *operation* is transformed: formerly strategic, it becomes surgical. This meaning, further-more, is clearly legible in the *Contre Sainte-Beuve* scene: "Then, in search of a pleasure that I did not know, I began to explore myself, and if I had been engaged in performing a surgical operation on my brain and marrow, I could not have been more agitated, more ter-rified. I believed at every moment that I should die" (CSB, 30). The guilt that accompanies the masturbatory act does not in the least arouse the anxiety that his body may be mutilated, that he may lose his penis. The attack the Narrator fears is directed against his personal identity ("marrow," "brain"); in fantasy, this menace is a lobotomy. "Death" completes the depersonalization, the dissolu-tion of his being. Since, as we have seen, the adolescent seeks the assurance of his "personality" (CSB, 31) in orgasm, the suppression of this personality is the worst kind of punishment.

In the same way the constant fear of the Narrator of the *Re-cherche* that he is not a "genius," not a "writer," clearly indicates his fear of passing away before he can stamp his individuality on the work, before he can become known and recognized as *unique* by the Other. Writing is here given the task of assuring that in-dependence—that autonomy, in the symbolic register—which a neurotic structure prohibits at the level of existence. By "becoming *I*," by waiting "to be" only "*I*," the writer thinks he is constructing a discourse in which the origin of speech coincides with the source of being. This enterprise is impossible for two reasons. If "I" refers to the linguistic act that utters it, hardly uttered, it splits into dis-tinct instances: "I" referent, "I" reference. Even in "first person," the narrative, like the Narrator, *is born of two*. But it is more than this. If "*I* refers to the act of individual discourse in which it is pronounced, and by this designates the speaker" (PGL, 226), reference is *purely linguistic:* "the reality to which it refers is the reality of discourse" (PGL, 226).

We might say that the Narrator's drama is lexical tragedy. Eliminating his proper noun (name) for the benefit of his pronoun, he thinks he is playing at "the loser wins." But the "I" turns back upon him; while the proper name normally has a referent in the real, while it designates this unique being which the Proustian quest seeks, the pronoun is self-referential, an empty form that can be located at the level of language, not of existence. Each of us is "I" from the instant we speak. In the order of the real, "I" is, by definition, *anyone*. If the anxiety about castration in the Narrator is given as a fear of losing identity, we can say that the suppression of the name-of-the-father constitutes the *castration of the son*.

The Narrator wants to become not simply a writer but a *famous* writer. To be "famous" means what? "To make a name for yourself." Now what the Narrator is least able to do is to make a name for himself, because he is, by choice, anonymous. At the very most he can try to make a first name for himself: "As soon as she was able to speak she said: 'My ——' or 'My dearest ——' followed by my christian name, which, if we give the narrator the same name as the author of this book, would be, 'My Marcel,' or 'My dearest Marcel'" (II, 429). There is no coquetry in this presumptive naming ("if we give"). The hesitation to identify the author and the Narrator is not pretense; it is real (we know that Proust, in his letters, at times admits and at times denies that the "I" is he). There is good reason for this: the "author of the book" (whose name is printed in full on the cover, Marcel Proust) cannot, in principle, *be* the "narrator," since one has a real referent and the other only a symbolic reference. Strictly speaking, they can be *homonyms* (a cat or bird can also be called Marcel), but they cannot be *identical*—thus, *identifiable*—in terms of being. This explains, moreover, that the "author" can be the writer of the book which has been "written"; the "narrator," that of the book "to be written"—the separation of the instances allowing this temporal disjunction. (Like their "authors," the two books can be homologues; they cannot be analogues.) Without a patronymic, without a totem, "I" is unnamable. Designating an inaccessible origin, it is the place where discourse simultaneously emerges and escapes.

With an art more perverse than Beckett's, the writer in Proust has created his own infernal machine. Just as "Aunt Léonie," as a result of living her death, finished by "dying" her life, *fictive anonymity*—a mask that the writer could remove—is transformed, in spite of him, into *actual anonymity*. We witness the fantasizer caught in the fantasy. Thanks to a certain confusion, the signatory, Marcel Proust, can gain access to the relative immortality he desires, but this can in no way be the immortality of "I." "I," by definition, cannot be "famous," because to be "famous" is—as we say so appropriately—to be "someone," and "I" is precisely *no one*. "I" may be the place in discourse where an existence makes itself known, but to the extent that the latter is not *named*, "I" remains *without reference*. By identifying with the mother to become his own Mother and to give birth to himself in language, in the desire for autofecundation, the writer suppresses the name-of-the-father: this suppression suppresses him as a writer. "The Son Who Belongs to No One," according to D. Fernandez's accurate analysis, his work-child will be the daughter who belongs to no one. The final status of the *Recherche* will be anonymous discourse from an anonymous source. The ablation of the name transforms the writer into the Narrator; the castration is finally assumed: the Narrator is the *castrated* writer. If the punishment feared for the masturbatory transgression is the loss of identity (CSB, 30), and if the act of writing is modeled upon the very act of masturbation (CSB, 31), as we have seen in the preceding pages, an unconscious logic demands that the *act of writing* be *punished by the loss of identity*. Thus writing is the occasion for a double self-punishment. The writer "expiates" the "murder of the mother" (devouring, ingestion, assimilation, use after death) by situating his activity in bodily suffering. The writer pays for the "murder of the father" (castration of the name) with his moral person. This first person, in which he lodges his *recherche*, dooms him to the impersonal.

Here we are perhaps touching upon the motivation behind the system of "perpetual reversals" that constitutes Proust's work. The *conscious project* (to find identity in writing) is exactly the *opposite of unconscious desire* (to be punished for writing by the loss of identity). In this regard, the madeleine scene is exemplary. At the moment when he believes he has located his identity in being, the Narrator refuses it any place in language. The compromise between the two conflictual tendencies makes the "Petites Madeleines" emerge. The scene in fact acts as a matrix, as the Narrator claims: "the whole . . . sprang into being." We may say that the entire book is constructed on this model. Conscious project: here is the book I want to write (*Temps retrouvé*). Unconscious desire: the book I have written is not mine; I am incapable of writing a book (*Du coté de chez Swann* to the *Temps retrouvé*). Result: loss of identity of the book which, like the instance that begets it, is strictly speaking *not identifiable*. Criticism struggles to decide whether the book which has just been read is the one which is announced: that is, whether there is *one* book or *two* (if the text "is born of one or of two," "the same is born of the same, or of another?"). The same fantasy of autofecundation governs the fate of the articulation (problematic of "I") and that of the totality of what is articulated (the written book). The text can be *attributed to no one*, not even to "I," since from the first page to the last the Narrator *has not begun to write. The Recherche* is actually the book Flaubert dreamed about, the book that "functions all by itself," the *anonymous book*.

Naturally, well-intentioned souls, who are legion (and it is out of well-intentioned souls that biographers are made), will remind us of the obvious: this is a fiction; in reality the text was written by Marcel Proust. Well-intentioned souls (who do not necessarily make good critics) forget one thing: the real, in fiction, is the fictional. If Marcel Proust is in the text, he managed to construct a verbal machine such that his discourse itself contains the point at which the discourse emerges and such that, in principle, the linguistic instance that utters it, "I," is cut off from all identifiable reference. We can, moreover, be reassured. Since "I" is anyone, it can *also*—even, if this will make the historians happy, *above all*—be Maurois's Marcel Proust or Painter's (a character as fictional as Swann or Charlus, who, like them, has only a textual existence). "I" is just as much the indefinitely open series of each new "reader of himself." If Marcel Proust comes first here, this must be understood as the madeleine indicates, as something to be repressed. Lifting the repression by analysis is not to uncover the illusion of this repression but to justify its meaning. The signatory shows us how not to read his book: by identifying him with the Narrator. Such a reading is possible, but it is a misreading. If the writer has taken care to strip the Narrator of his particular traits, to take his descriptive I.D. from him, it is because of neither literary strategy nor personal shyness. Staging the story of "I," he has retained only those details that can account for this *unique passion to be "I"*; he has "thinned out" his narrative in the direction of a kind of pronominal transparency. What is articulated mimes the fictional articulation: in opposition to the "fatty layer" with which he thickens Charlus, he "trims" the Narrator.

The writer's fantasy, as Aunt Léonie gave it to us, was "*I have being, so others don't have it.*" The necessities of writing split this fantasy open: "*I*" *has only linguistic being.* The source of Logos is of the order of Logos. Being cannot be transported into the written word. The generalized reversal of signs (reversals of all kinds, the fundamental instability which makes of the literary object that is the *Recherche*—according to Sartre's term—the "spinning top" par excellence) undoubtedly originates in this irreducible opposition between conscious project (to be yourself) and unconscious desire (not to be yourself): that is, at the level of expression, in the radical divergence between the end and the means of the work. "We find fault with the 'water' of a stone, or with the words of a sentence because they are not fashioned exclusively from the spirit of a fleeting intimacy and of a 'loss unparalleled'" (i, 167). The dreamer of names attempts to restore this "fleeting intimacy" (*essence*) to signs; he wants to be the redresser of language. By means of an instrument (language) that knows only the general, the writer has as his aim the capture of what is singular; the *three* Martinville towers, Albertine's *ten* faces.

From this point of view, proliferation in the Proustian sentence has a denotative intention that orients the whole system of connotation. Once you have assigned them a kind of descriptive exhaustiveness, you can no longer arrest the flux of words. There will never be enough words to say everything about a single experience. Proustian writing exhausts itself by reaching for this particularity that escapes—sensations, gestures, intentions, glances, and words. In this regard the theory, like the practice of "metaphor," constitutes proof of failure, since in any case it takes *two* to express the *one*. The more it tries to grasp a "unicity," the more it seems that writing shifts. The system of the deictics (I, here, now), normally destined to furnish discourse with points of reference, is precisely what sets it afloat: we will never know *who* speaks *where* and *when* in Proustian discourse. We might say that of all the "tombs" in his cemetery, the Narrator has chosen the most empty one for himself. The self-punishment is radical. If the *projected* (conscious) book is (unconsciously) an imaginary resolution of an Oedipal complex, the book *actually written* is a confrontation with an *actual castration*. We are inclined to think that the Narrator has gone too far. As a result of wanting to free himself from subjection to obtain, as subject, his own being, he has taken the *operation* literally. He has effected a real ablation out of a symbolic separation. Wanting to make a *unique* name for himself, he has become *anonymous*.

◀ I I ▶

The writer's bad faith would, in the end, be unmasked by the truth of writing—the ultimate tragedy of a work that is perhaps more tragic than all others. Giving shape to the work, fantasy would follow the same path as writing: the book would constitute *the writing of fantasy* to reveal more effectively *the fantasy of writing*. Giving birth to yourself in language, (re)producing yourself in the symbolic are only mystified desires. The writer will need to accept writing as the location of his own lack. Finally, the long path we have tried to follow would be understood as the particular way in which Proustian fantasy plays with the law of writing and is played in it, a law that has been incisively and decisively formulated by Jacques Derrida: "This fact bears on what we have proposed about the essence of the energy of the *graphein* as the originary efface-ment of the proper name. From the moment that the proper name is erased in a system, there is writing, there is a "subject" from the moment that this obliteration of the proper is produced, that is to say from the first appearing of the proper and from the first dawn of language."[34] This is the status of a literature that is post-Oedipal, "adult," rid of the dual mother-child obsession, which fantasy transposes into the relation of the author to his text. "I" would thus get the better of Proust, would turn against Proust.

It would be easy to stop with this conclusion. We recognize the theoretical discourses of today: absence of the subject, work with-out an author, impersonality of literature or, better, deconstruc-tion of "literature" as an "ideological" concept, and whatever else you like. Of course, there is *some* truth in these theories. But if there is some truth, it is because there is also some untruth. If we immobilize the "spinning top" that is the literary work, it falls. The game, the toy of words, exists only if it spins all the time. No more could literary than clinical analysis be a kind of comprehen-sion that is fixed; at the same time, it is always "terminated, inter-minable." To confuse a moment of a dialectic with its *resolution* is absurd: "Literature is made up of moments which are different, dis-tinct from each other, which oppose each other. Honesty, which is analytical because it wants to see clearly, separates them."[35] But Blanchot is putting us on our guard. What is separated must be reunited, not in a "synthesis" in which "oppositions" would be resolved in the Hegelian transparency of the concept, but in the union of *contraries* that are *dialectically insoluble:*

The writer must at the same time respond to several absolute and ab-solutely different commandments, and his morality is made up of the encounter and opposition of implacably hostile rules. . . . One says to him: "You will not write, you will remain nothingness, you will keep silent, you will be ignorant of words." The other: "Know only words." "Write to say nothing." "Write to say something." "No work, but the experience of yourself, the knowledge of what is unknown to you." "A work. A real work, recognized by others and important to others." "Efface the reader." "Efface yourself in front of the reader." [PF, 315–16]

Proust was certainly aware of these contradictory "commandments," a few of which are given to us by Blanchot. We could say that he experienced them to the point of martyrdom.

Where do we find these contradictory "commandments" that we nevertheless have to find a way to obey? Where do we find, in regard to a single object, the simultaneous presence of insurmountable relations of opposition? If the writer must "make a work" and "not make a work," "efface the reader" and "efface himself in front of the reader," where can we find these acts in two movements, the first of which is "annulled" by the second? Where, if not in the model of *obsessional neurosis*, which Freud tells us is that of religion and art? Compulsion, ambivalence, retroactive annulment— the mechanisms of neurosis define just as precisely the laws of literary production. If (as Freud tells us in *The Future of an Illusion*), like the obsessional neurosis of children, cultural neuroses are caught in the Oedipal complex and in the relationship to the father (repression of the "secret" of the "primitive murder," the historic— or mythic—counterpart of the death wish), then Proust's work is completely inscribed within the structure of neurosis. But one must point out that far from being a *deliverance* from that structure, his work attests to it as a *truth that cannot be transcended*. We take leave of Freud when, in his praiseworthy concern to "distinguish" the artist's neurosis in the face of the sempiternal accusation of reductionism, he occasionally comes to take art for a liberation from fantasy, the triumph of the work of sublimation over brute impulses; when he at times sees in artistic creation a way to avoid neurosis, a kind of spontaneous "cure."[36] For in the case of neurosis, art liberates, sublimates, avoids, cures nothing; it is completely *neurotic passion*. If this study has a purpose, it is to show that at all levels (conception of literature, techniques of narration or of writing—not to speak, of course, of obvious themes), fantasy does not condition, give shape to, construct, or deconstruct the work; at the limit, it *is* the work.

At the limit, only; the achieved or achievable significance cannot be confused with the movement of its genesis. That is to say the *Recherche* calls for or demands other kinds of readings than those of its archeology of fantasy; the study of narrativity, of style, and—why not—of sociology and history are necessary and irreplaceable. If you choose, you can read the *Recherche* like Revel, as a document of the age. As in cooking, in criticism there is something for everyone—as long as you see that whatever the metalanguage used, there is no ultimate decoding of the metaphorical language of the work into a rigorously metonymic language that would "lay out" its meaning. We must say of literary discourse what Lévi-Strauss says of mythic discourse: "The unity of the myth is never more than tendential and projective and cannot reflect a state or a particular moment of the myth. It is a phenomenon of the imagination, resulting from the attempt at interpretation; and its function is to endow the myth with synthetic form and to prevent its disintegration into a confusion of opposites."[37]

Such is, for us, the essential function of analytic interpretation; the Oedipal schema allows us to subsume the partial tendencies, the contradictory movements, the complementary but disjointed moments of unconscious discourse within a synthetic structure without which pure discontinuity would be simple incoherence. We must, however, admit that criticism constructs its interpretation "within the Oedipal complex," as the child organizes his or her behavior there or as the patient replays his or her actions there. Interpretation, according to Lévi-Strauss's remark on myths—and the analytic Oedipal complex is one—is an "imaginary phenomenon." All of the categories used to codify the language of desire and of anxiety, identification, projection, castration have no foundation in a "real" situated beneath "illusion"; the only real you ever reach here (unlike that of a biological explanation) is imaginary.

We should analyze the language of analysis; so ready to "demystify" other discourses, it needs to demystify itself. Were we to look closely (which we cannot do, of course, in these few remarks), we would see that despite its aspiration to scientific status, analytic language is not, or is only partly, a true metalanguage. In fact, it participates in a fundamental way in metaphorical language, which it attempts to resolve into a discourse that is strictly metonymic. More precisely, the articulations of psychoanalytic discourse are on the order of logical discourse, capable of functioning with all the rigor of a metalanguage and of being manipulated as such. But the concepts that lay the foundation on which the theory rests are disguised metaphors: "instances" introduced by a comparison with the courts; a "psychic apparatus" analogous to an optical apparatus, whose different "systems" light penetrates; "repression" represented by a watchman who stands at the threshold between two rooms. To introduce his key concepts, Freud often uses what he calls "auxiliary representations."[38]

I find no fault with this, except that from the point of view of the constitution of a scientific metalanguage, the concept can never be recuperated from the comparison used to introduce it. When Freud writes: "The ego covers the id only with its surface which is formed by the system Pcs., almost as the germinal disc covers the egg,"[39] the theory remains founded upon this "almost." From the "economic" point of view (based upon the consideration of displacements of an "energy" which we are told is of a quantitative order although not currently measurable) or from the "topical" point of view (which according to Laplanche and Pontalis supposes "a differentiation of the psychical apparatus into a certain number of systems . . . which enables us to consider them metaphorically as psychical locations to which we can give a spatial representation"),[40] the theoretical discourse of psychoanalysis does not ultimately go beyond the level of *natural language*, into which, in defining itself, it is immediately translated. Projected upon the axis of metonymy, it is organized into a rigorously logical chain and proposes models of transformation having properties that adequately take into account the matter under study (we have, on our part, tried to verify this in our "construction" of the *Recherche*, using the madeleine as the point of departure). Upon its other axis, however, the discourse of the analysis of metaphor—in opposition to that of linguistics—remains caught in metaphor; here, it is not a question of a difference of "value" or "method" between the two disciplines but simply of the fact that one by necessity *includes*, the other *excludes*, in its discourse the *subject* of the discourse. One catches hold of the speaker in his or her language; the other offers itself a language without a speaker. If, according to Benveniste, "Ego is who Ego says," the subject cannot speak itself outside of the metaphorical dimension, within which it entirely constructs itself.

In other words, a discourse *on* the unconscious, however objective it may wish to be, remains a discourse *of* the unconscious. This is a fundamental contradiction, an inverse double postulation of analytic language, which is often disguised by Freudian "clarity" but which calls (even cries) out for attention, in Lacanian discourse; the tormented faithfulness to the unconscious becomes at one end spoonerism, at the other end diagram, and is permanently split between graph and graffiti. Freud himself, the Freud of Eros and Thanatos, of Logos and Anankè, eventually gives his metapsychology the dimension of a mythology; if he is always "fascinated" by poets, it is because analysis is actually constituted as a *poetics* (the laws of the discourse of the unconscious). If, however, the unconscious is structured like a language, we must add that language is structured like the unconscious. Above and beyond the discourse of the *analyst*, traditionally included in the analytic situation indirectly in the well-known "countertransference," the discourse of the *analysis* must also be integrated within it; a cultural discourse, it too is caught in the neurotic structure that it sets free, without itself becoming set free. It is in no way situated "outside" the neurosis or beyond "illusion." Or, rather, it is precisely its neurosis to believe it is escaping neurotic structures; its fantasy, to believe it is dissipating fantasy. The actual history of analysis is inscribed within its own imaginary; it's a mortal rivalry—in each generation (every time), "sons" of Oedipus-Freud once again kill the father (Freud, moreover, having instituted analysis by means of the symbolic murder of his own father, obsessionally replayed from "Dostoevsky" to "Moses").

It is interesting to notice that one major piece of the theory, the phallus as signifier of *both* sexes, is strenuously criticized by a new American school, which sees in it a projection of Freudian anti-feminism and a misunderstanding of a specifically feminine sexuality (which Jones had a sense of a long time ago). Orthodox analysts respond that these critics simply reveal, through their misunderstanding of the phallus, the fantasies of "feminism." Whether the fantasies are feminist or Freudian matters little; the essential thing is that sexuality belongs to the order of fantasy. Sex is not a raw given, a fact that is "real"—for example, biological; it is constituted at the end of a series of imaginary identifications. The homosexual who, to use a very hypothetical case, is led in the course of his treatment to stop identifying with the mother and to identify with the father would not discover his "true" sex at all; to change identifications is to exchange one for another. To rework the identification system is in no way to abolish it. In this sense, and whatever the uncontestable validity of the models of comprehension it offers us, analytic discourse never enables us to emerge from the illusory domain of symptom or symbol onto the "ground" of a real that would be neither symptom nor symbol. It helps us to redistribute symptoms, to reconvert symbols; it can rearticulate our fantasies, but it cannot enable us to "depart from" the imaginary register that is the mode of the human psyche's being.

If, then, according to Lévi-Strauss, the effort of interpretation gives a synthetic form to myth to prevent it from dissolving into the "confusion of opposites," it does not mean that the contradiction is finally surmounted or suppressed. The purpose of these few cursory remarks, and of this perspective on a complex field—which could rightfully be termed cavalier—is simply to determine the significance of this field in the conclusion of our study. In literary criticism, the psychoanalytic approach is often accused of being "reductive." It can be; there is the well-known "only" that seems to constitute the personal pleasure of the analyst (the sadistic type) in his role of "demystifier," more than it constitutes the purpose of an analytic explication. The critic makes himself the text's super-ego: I am the father; the writer is the child. We have the English saying: "Father knows best." We can be almost sure of meeting this "only" in all psychoanalytic criticism (including this). I open a book at random and find Freud, concluding his study of Michel-angelo: the enormous statue, with its prodigious physical power, "is no more than" the concrete expression of the greatest accom-plishment of the human spirit—to triumph over passion in the name of a cause to which you are devoted (a beautiful example, if ever there was one, of projection). Or Mauron, in his *Introduction à la psychanalyse de Mallarmé:* "The page is nothing other than the window."[41] Every analytic situation, vis-à-vis a person or a work, brings with it its own transferences.

Obviously, the present study does not escape this rule. It is caught in the very structure it claims to discover in Proust. It pro-ceeds by *identification* ("I am Proust," as the Narrator says; "I am my mother") and by *murder* ("to be me, as a critic, I kill Proust," as the Narrator says; "to be me, as a writer, I kill Mamma"). Here we find again precisely the *two movements* of retroactive annul-ment: criticism, a cultural discourse, is in its turn a form of obses-sional neurosis; and analytic interpretation enters fully into the system of fantasy it reveals. (In this regard it is instructive to see that in a work on Freud's aesthetic that is otherwise very well in-formed and intelligent, *L'Enfance de l'art*, by S. Kofman, the author constantly repeats, "To be done with an ideological conception of art, you have to kill the Father," without perceiving that she is adding softly, "as Dad says.") In brief, if we have tried to show how the *Recherche* emerges from fantasy, beginning with those things that are latent in the madeleine, criticism does not enable *us* to emerge from it. It settles us there, but this time with complete awareness. After all, what else has the analytic procedure ever done?

We have, then, in no way "demystified" Proust. Or, rather, we have to demystify our own demystification. By underlining that the linguistic narcissism of "I" relegates the scriptor to the realm of the impersonal, we have not indicated a hidden contradiction in the

Narrator that an opportune moment of lucidity can resolve; the contradiction is in language, where a speaker, by the very act with which he would like to designate his own person in the real world, refers only to his grammatical person in discourse. When we oppose the writer's fantasy, "I control being," to the truth of writing, "There is no being in language," we do not come up with an illusion that the appropriate propaedeutic will dissipate. The Narrator simply lives, in his own way, the impossibility of all literary creation, which assumes either complicity between language and reference ("realistic" literature) or a motivating relation between signifier and signified ("poetic" writing)—congruences and similarities that linguistics reveals to be mythic and literature claims to be necessary. We take at random three (supposedly) nonneurotic theoreticians, and we read:

A writer of prose or any writer, when he speaks of a table, writes a few words on this table, but he writes them really in such a way—according to his purely subjective idea—that this verbal whole is a kind of reproduction or production of the table, so that the table in a way enters the words.[42]

This realism (in the scholastic sense of the term) which demands that names be the "reflection" of ideas, takes on a radical form in Proust, but we may ask ourselves whether it is not more or less consciously present in every act of writing, and if it is actually possible to be a writer without believing, in a certain way, in a natural relationship between names and essences. [NEC, 134]

Things and words were to be separated from one another. . . . Discourse was still to have the task of speaking that which is, but it was no longer to be anything more than what it said. . . . and yet, throughout the nineteenth century, and right up to our own day. . . . literature achieved autonomous existence, and separated itself from all other languages with a deep scission, only by forming a sort of "counter-discourse," and by finding its way back from the representative or signifying function of language to this raw being that had been forgotten since the sixteenth century.[43]

We *know* that the mimesis of writing is an illusion; that the motivation of signs is an illusion; that a realistic semiology is without a scientific foundation. These things are myths. Exactly—literary activity functions within a mythic structure, in the precise sense that myth is here to resolve and, failing in this, to veil contradictions. It consists in acting *as if* the impossible (in the real) were possible, and in fact *it becomes so* (in the imaginary). A personal myth takes the form of a neurosis. If the Narrator is a neurotic, he can become a writer, because literature—itself a paradigm of contrary postulations—is completely caught within a neurotic structure. To write is not, as the theory would lead you too hastily to conclude, "to emerge" from neurosis in the least; it is to adhere to it. There is simply a conversion from one level to another within the same system; in fact the Narrator lodges his enterprise of liberation in the very location of his most intimate servitude through inversion: "For a long time I used to go to bed early" becomes "sleeping by day/working by night." If the new activity is inscribed within the childhood habitus, it is precisely because literature is an adult infantilism.

In his article of 1908, "The Relation of the Poet to Day-Dreaming," Freud demonstrates in a remarkable way the substitutive relation between the games the child plays with the world and those of the poet with words: "So when the human being grows up, and ceases to play, he only gives up the connection with real objects; instead of playing, he then begins to create fantasy."[44] The fundamental fantasy or, better, the fantasy that lays the foundation for the writer—what we might call the *impulse to write*—this fantasy can be found, I believe—as much as or even more than in the latent thoughts of diurnal dreams, where Freud situates it (ambitious and erotic wishes)—at the level of the *very relationship to language*. This relationship may be seen as a gamelike illusion of verbal creativity, a nostalgia for which remains in the adult. The relationship, clearly indicated by Proust ("As a matter of fact, we each derived a certain amount of satisfaction from the mannerism, being still at the age in which we believe that one gives a thing a real existence by giving it a name"; I, 61), is well-defined by Sartre:

"In every writer, there is a childhood side which does not have communication as its purpose, and which is precisely creation-appropriation: creating the 'table' through words" (s, 43).

But the desire is not only to capture things in words, nor is the desire only the writer's, if it is true—as Merleau-Ponty says—that every act of expression implies "the vow to retrieve the world taken with the first appearance of a language, that is, with the first appearance of a finite system of signs which claimed to be capable in principle of winning by a sort of ruse any being which might present itself."[45] A remark that Benveniste makes in passing undoubtedly gives us what is specific in the writer's desire: "Language is so organized that it permits each speaker to *appropriate to himself* an entire language by designating himself as *I*" (PGL, 226).

Beyond the imaginary "creation" of things is the *appropriation of words*. If this purpose is also common to all speakers, the ordinary speaker or writer is generally content with a practical appropriation, with an efficient manipulation; we say quite fittingly that someone "possesses" a language. The writer, however, takes this wish for possession literally; his ultimate desire as writer, in modern times at least, is to make of *a* language *his very own* language. La Bruyère admits it explicitly, at the beginning of our history. From the word go, from the first chapter of the *Caractères*,[46] between the initial aporia ("Everything has been said, and we've arrived too late") and the final response ("but I said it my own way"), the purpose of the impulse to write is revealed: to use the words of others as *your own*. Once again, need is located in an obsessional demand. *It wants the impossible*. Whatever I do, my words are always those of other people; language is the Other as a code. My expressive possibilities are rigorously limited by a system whose constraints govern all levels of my discourse, from simple phonological play to narrative verisimilitude; I generate neither my lexicon nor my syntax. Saying whatever it may be *as my own*, if I want to be *understood*, is precisely what I can do least.

Also, then, the phantasmagoria by means of which the Narrator "eats" his mother to become "Aunt Léonie," or by means of which he becomes "his own mother" to give birth to the "child-book," are by no means illusions of which the science of analysis will finally clear the work; the phantasmatic Narrative is *the only true story* of the Narrator's literary vocation. It is born where every birth takes place: *inter urinam et faeces nascimur*—between tea and madeleine. The dual relationship to the mother, the fascinated ambivalence, the intermingling of love-hate, the fundamental impossibility of being yourself with or without the Other—these are not the ultimate anecdotal "complexes" of the Narrator, which the *Recherche* tells us about. But through the writer's complexes, which are accidental, it reveals those complexes of writing that are essential.

Proust's ability to join the absolute individuality of a single destiny and project with the very essence of the literary enterprise clearly reveals how remarkably exemplary he is. For the modern writer necessarily replays with *language* the scenario that the Narrator plays with his mother—with the Other, from whom he issues. If every language is a mother tongue to the extent that our own language is generated out of it (where our possibilities for expression are inscribed and consigned in advance; we could say they are "coded," in the sense of a code that is as much genetic as it is linguistic), the writer's desire for "originality," beyond the ostentatious facade, attempts to recuperate the origin; to be *original* is to make yourself or to want yourself to be *the origin*. No one understands this better than Proust when he tells us that Vinteuil "reached his own essential nature at those depths, where, whatever be the question asked, it is in the same accent, that is to say its own, that it replies" (II, 558). An opposing tendency in the writer, *destruction-appropriation*, completes the process of *creation-appropriation* described by Sartre. "To be yourself," to find "the same accent, [your] own," you must conquer your in-dependence, like the child over the Mother; and similarly, your own being is affirmed in and through a "tearing away," a rupture. If our essence is to take on a *form* of language, in the realm of language we can *form* nothing that does not obey the inflexible rule of the code; we can only *deform*. Our own being can be inscribed only in the play of differences of a system that is defined in advance—something that students of stylistics clearly see when they distinguish "style" as a *deviation* with respect to a norm. We must now restore the disruptive thrust to this "stylistic deviation." To differ is to do violence. Distortion is aggression.

The desire to write is a form of the impulse to dominate. We understand better why and how the Narrator's neurotic failure to find his own being in the real (subjection to his mother) can be converted into an imaginary success (mastery of the mother tongue). What we have empirically demonstrated in regard to the reading scene—the relations which form around *François le Champi* in the triad mother-child-language—can no doubt be integrated within a general framework. We must take our thesis to its logical conclusion. If literature, like everything that culture produces, is caught in an obsessional structure, it must be able to be constructed upon the same theoretical model. In his 1913 article, "The Disposition to Obsessional Neurosis," Freud demonstrated the importance of the sadistic and anal-erotic impulses in the clinical picture: "The component-impulses which govern this *pregenital* organization of the sexual life are, moreover, the anal-erotic and sadistic impulses."[47] We find precisely these two contrary impulses, which Freud organizes into an opposition between the passive (anal) and the active (sadistic), at work in the constitution of Proustian writing. Summoned by the mother-marquise in the *chalet de necessité* (the water-closet) to *make*, in his struggle for mastery the Narrator *refuses;* in place of this, as we have said, he *will make* Combray. But so that Combray can be made *in this place* (which is also that of the digested madeleine and of the act of masturbation), writing must take on the value of the *execution of a refusal* (opposed, let us remember, to the mother's offer of tea in the madeleine scene, and also to the mother's image in the masturbation scene). Literary *activity* is the form taken, at the level of language, by this "general instinct to mastery" that Freud discusses, which wants to subdue the object even to the point of destroying it and which compensates, at this archaic level, for the *passivity* of the *anal* condition. Just as the child makes himself independent, anally, by rejecting the maternal order, the writer takes possession of his autonomy by rejecting linguistic injunctions. To write is to refuse to "make" on command. In this way the rupture with the mother tongue, the transgression of the code of the Other, takes place. Proust, so prompt to track down the offenses of all his characters against the word, to catalogue the distortions they cause it to undergo, conceals in this way his own fundamental transgression: the violence that lays the foundation of and establishes his existence as a writer.

We are familiar with Paul Souday's well-known remark when *Swann* appeared: "It is swarming with errors." Paul Souday was right. The original writer (in modern times, the writer, in short) by definition *writes badly*, since he does not write "like other people." This is obvious from Balzac to Proust. The Academy had already had occasion to point this out to Corneille, and its enemies said the same to Racine. You can be "original" only by deviating from the norm; you can manifest your "own accent" only by means of a difference in the code. Thus, for the writer desiring to appropriate language, the property of words demands the impropriety of style. Unable to *form* anything that is "your own," you can, according to La Bruyère's formula, "say in your own way" only what you *de-form*—and La Bruyère is the best practitioner of his theory. Proust, moreover, said it all when he said that the best way to "defend" the French language is to "attack it."[48] By means of secondary fantasies only, the oral-sadistic impulse, manifest in the devouring of the mother-madeleine, ultimately underlies the impulse to write: "eating his mother to become his own mother in the form of Aunt Léonie." Orality can certainly be the place for linguistic aggression (words that you "murder" like the director of the Grand-Hotel or Françoise, or "swallow" like Saniette, etc.).

But orality cannot be the final battlefield of the instinct for mastery. If I try to be understood by others when I speak, I have to speak *like them*. The need for immediate communication attenuates all particularity of expression—if, of course, it does not annul it; orally, you are "original" by your tics (Albertine's slang or Saint-Loup's phraseology): that is, simply by words from *another* group that you transport into your own. Like the vocables it employs, this originality is only a *borrowing* and therefore comes to an end of itself. This is why we hardly ever hear the *Recherche*'s Narrator: to be different from others, he must *never speak*. Or rather, if you manage to "be yourself" through speech, it is because like Charlus you write, so to speak, out loud; the actual originality of an oral language is failed writing. The fine conversationalist, Swann or Charlus, is a would-be writer.

For the Proustian Narrator then, writing is not silent speech; it participates in another order of expression that is implied but not explained here. If "conversation" is constantly decried as a turning away from the self, it is because as a subject, you are never "yourself" in a speech which is invested—and travestied—by your being-for-the-other. At the level of analysis, we could say that the need for an original language, which is a desire to be the origin of language, cannot be assigned to the oral stage (even if it were oral-sadistic, as in Abraham). The mouth is the place for input. It can refuse to open, but it does not have control over what comes to pass there. As aggressive as it is, mastication does not reject; by swallowing what it is given, it endorses it. It absorbs without producing. We might think that it is otherwise with speech, since we do produce that. Rather we should say that we reproduce it. Speaking (or writing in the banal sense) is a purely mimetic gesture. My speech is the speech of the Other—what I think I am constituting, I am restoring—whereas writing, whatever the norms to which it is submitted, tends (according to Proust's remark) toward "its unique accent, its very own." Your own oral language, whatever the individual variables, is the one you speak "without an accent."

With remarkable certainty, Proustian fantasy situates writing at the anal stage. The passivity of oral absorption (nutritive, linguistic) is compensated for by the control of the *output*. You master evacuation by taking on once again the responsibility of "matter"; it is because of a lack of this material inscription that the speaker, contrary to the scriptor, cannot leave a "trace," a "mark," on language. Certainly the exit as much as the entrance is a place for training; civilization is repression. It is at this very point that the most severe seizure by the Other occurs. In both the natural and symbolic orders, to command, you first have to obey. Independence is achieved in the end in the refusal to obey. "To say in your own way," is to manage "to make in your own way," substituting linguistic matter for fecal matter. Seizing control from the material Other, decivilizing yourself, when you "make" your work as the writer, you "de-make" (defecate) language as you like. Freud declares in a well-known passage that writing, "which consists in allowing a fluid to flow out from a tube upon a piece of white paper," can take on the signification of a coitus,[49] as our analysis of the *Contre Sainte-Beuve* text exemplifies. Proust gives us a yet more distant truth: if the madeleine scene (matrix of the work) is superimposable upon *two* complementary scenes—of masturbation in the first text, but also of defecation in the Champs-Elysées text—Proustian fantasy shows through the superimposition of models that if coitus occurs in writing, it is anal coitus.

The whole phantasmagoria of writing is ultimately rearticulated at this level. In the transformational series, if it is true that the anal-sadistic stage is not only the precursor of the genital stage but—the genital function having been fulfilled—can succeed and dissolve it ("The Disposition to Obessional Neurosis," 94), we have the cause of this "regression" in the fact that the obsessional structure in which literature, like culture, is inscribed implies a fixation at the anal stage. Whatever we make of these clinical considerations, the important thing is to try to see how this mythic object, the "literary object," is constituted and functions. Because if "fantastic literature" is actually a literary "genre," then in one sense there is *only* a literature of fantasy. Proust—and this is perhaps one of the reasons for the fascination he exercises—demonstrates that those texts "reworked" most by a conscious stylist are, in fact, written in the dialectics of the unconscious, where we know that contraries coexist without canceling each other out. This is, indeed, the language of literature whose fundamental contradictions are not spread out in a smooth series, as a (superficial) reading of the quoted text by Blanchot would have us believe, but form a circle of symbolic equivalences that are presented in this circuit of the anal.

Creation-appropriation: these two movements, which in their

retroactive annulment punctuate the relationship of the writer to language, also mark the relationship of the anus to the world, through which eroticism is alternately retention and evacuation, a sadism that possesses and eliminates the object. This activity is guilty in itself, in terms of the symbolic law that civilizes. If, as we were saying, in making the work the writer "de-makes" (defecates) language as he chooses, in the eyes of the Other—mother-nourishment, mother-tongue, mother-country—the writer "makes" badly. Mallarmé and Proust are not "French"; *Finnegans Wake* is no longer English; but Racine was already often "improper."

It is a fact; the accent proper to you is improper. Such is the rebellious child, clenched in constipation or fleeing in diarrhea (Mallarmé or Proust), the one who "makes" badly is "bad." This evildoer is a malefactor; we know to what extent every society watches over such a person: "nourished" at one end with culture, the humanities, principles, and precepts with which this society is "chock-full", at the other end the writer makes of this the very "substance" of the self. What results is the curiously ambivalent status of the writer's product: "it's literature,"/"it's only literature"—an opposition in which the valorizing sign suddenly is devalorized and which if applied, for example, to science (it's science/it's only science) would have no relevance. A sacred object on one end, language as a finished product is excrement on the other. Its craft will be at one and the same time that of a god and a clown. If we pursue the cycle of symbolic equivalences, food can be said to be "my own" (my food) only by metonymy (it enters me). On the contrary, excrement is "me" by metaphor (it issues from me). The shit that I make is *my* shit. This is why, whereas I am given my food (my madeleine, my language), I can give you my feces (my work). The sadistic impulse becomes generous: your scybalum is your "gift"—we are familiar with this childhood trait.

But Mallarmé also makes us a "poem as gift." Or again we have the Baudelairean present—"I offer you these lines, so that if my name . . ."—where, in the signed gift, we find once again the "calling card," a trace of the poet's passage in language, analogous to the *grumus merdae* with which, as Freud reminds us, the burglar insists upon marking his break-in (CP, 386). The same text reminds us also that the feces are "the child," a fact that is immediately affirmed by Mallarmé's "gift" of the poem: "I bring to you the child of an Idumean night." At the end of Mallarmé's scriptural sadism, which (even more cruelly than Proust) dislocates, dismembers, and tortures letters and language, we discover the same anal birth of the book-child, a birth that is also the figuration of a cloacal coitus—if it is true that the pile of feces is also a "penis". In fact, the "conjunction" of Charlus and Jupien—the bumblebee's fertilization of the orchid, which is at one and the same time a model for the ultimate self-fertilization of the book and a unique *mise en scène* of intercourse in the *Recherche*—arouses "an immediate afterthought of cleanliness" (II, 9). In this way, for the Narrator, a double possibility takes shape around the feces-phallus: to be both mother and child, the subject and the object of birth. If, as we have seen above, the Narrator's desire in relation to the phallus is to have a castrated belly, rid of the penis-clamp, defecation offers an ideal prototype of castration (CP, 389), the assurance of a femininity that is renewed constantly and without pain: "an iron clamp left sticking in a statue that has been taken down from its niche" is now easily detached.

What you lose however, you regain. The Narrator, while at the same time being the mother, is the child, since he is his scybalum, his scybalum is his phallus, and the child is the mother's phallus. In a closely knit network, anality once more weaves, so to speak, all the fantasies into a new pattern. The preceding analyses can be regrouped into a symbolic unity: "Feces, child, penis constitute in this way a unity, an unconscious concept—*sia venia verbo*—the concept of a little thing which can be detached from the body" (CP, 389). The beautiful unity, however, of this hardly constituted "concept" suddenly dissolves—because the detachable object, both "me" and "not me," "loved" and "hated," bearing a fundamental ambivalence, is torn by a painful contradiction. Detaching itself from the body, the object is born, but in the very act, it dies. At the very moment that it leaves the cloacal matrix, the "gift" is transformed into waste. The gold (feces are also "money") becomes filth. Separated from the writer-excreter, the product, so patiently composed, decomposes. "Heat will withdraw from the earth, then life itself" (II, 507); grandiosely summoned by Proust, entropy is the allegory of an excremental destiny: "My books also, like my earthly being, would finally some day die" (II, 1120).

Perhaps it would be better to say that they begin with death. Curiously, in his meditation upon "Literature and the Right to Death," Blanchot follows an itinerary parallel to Freud's. Seeking the key to this "right of literature to indifferently assign each of its moments and each of its results a negative or a positive sign" (PF, 342), Blanchot finds it in the ambiguity with which life and death are articulated in language. Literature is "*this life which brings with it death and sustains itself in it. . . .* an alternative whose terms overlap in the ambiguity which makes them identical by making them contraries" (PF, 345). At the end of the symbolic Freudian circuit, expression-excretion also articulates the act of writing in the simultaneous contradiction of the impulse to life and the impulse to death, displaced from the obsessional psychic structure love-hate and projected in the cosmogonic dimension of Eros and Thanatos.

This digression or, if you prefer, "anal regression" (which is what I am not afraid to call the *critical fantasy*) was intended to show— by recoding in the discourse of the anal the fleeting and complex Proustian phantasmagoria—that if phantasmal language is plural, there is no other language to discuss the literary object, at least if we see it not in such and such a form but in the whirligig of its contrary postulations, in its totality—forever detotalized. When we said above that the Narrator's conscious project (to be himself) is the opposite of his unconscious desire (not to be himself), there was no conflict there that an appropriate *prise de conscience* could have resolved. If the greatest works actually possess the status of this "little thing which can be detached from the body," which Freud talks about, then the book-excrement, the book-child, the book-penis necessarily participates in the phantasmal status of a dismembered body.

In a curious recent text, Barthes opposes speech, which "is subject to remanence, it *smells*," to writing—which, he says, "does not smell: having been produced (having completed the process of production), it falls, not in the way that a bellows collapses, but in the way that a meteorite disappears; it travels far from my body and yet it is not a detached piece, withheld narcissistically, like speech; its disappearance is not deceptive; it passes, it crosses over, that's it."[50] Writing, it seems, will be spared the anal (olfactory) destiny reserved for a speech "narcissistically" withheld; writing "falls" and "travels" outside of the body but in a noble way, like a "meteorite." Such luminous speeding movement should erase all corporeal traces; the written text should be "liberated by writing." But this is not the case at all:

What bothers me about it is precisely that, dealing with speech, it cannot, in this very writing, liquidate speech completely. In order to write "on" speech (on the subject of speech), whatever the distance achieved in writing, I am obliged to refer to those illusions of experience, of memory, of sentiment which occur to the subject that I am when I speak, that I was when I spoke; in this writing, a referent still exists, and this is the scent which I myself pick up. [12]

In this remarkable text, in a personal fantasy (the Barthesian desire to rid the sign of reference), we have a cultural mythology: "liberated language," an "articulation" without an "articulated" or an "articulator," "scription" which will eliminate from itself all ties to speech—that is, to a register of language in which the presence of "I" in its discourse has recourse to an individual history (experiences, memories, sentiments). What is essential for our purposes is not the admission that as long as there continues to be speech in writing, an olfactory "remanence," an original trace, is difficult or impossible to "liquidate"; nor the consideration that the desire to erase the trace (odor) remains caught within the problematic of the trace itself (simply seen as bad, after having been pursued as good—and Proust's project is located precisely at this moment of ambivalence). What is important here seems to me to be that by introducing the entirely metaphorical notion of "the odor of speech," by opposing to it that of an *odorless* writing, and by inserting this writing in his metaphorical network, Barthes confers upon writing the very quality that he renounces. The disavowal is an avowal here; the negation, a denial. By his too persistent insistence in telling us that it does not smell, he only tells us (again) that *it smells*. And Barthes—with a whole wing of the avant-garde—knows not that it smells.

But what does it smell of, exactly? Unlike money, written words do not "talk." Spoken or written, words do not smell. What is the meaning of this metaphor? The passage from Barthes came to mind because it echoes the madeleine passage I am treating. Let us re-read this, then, one final time: "My mother . . . offered me some tea, a thing I did not ordinarily take." The scene is brought about, in fact, by the mother's remark, which produces an implicit conversation ("I declined at first"). The experience to which the remark leads tells us of the separation, then the reunion, and finally the memory of a "taste" and of something "visual." Now what is the obstacle to the remembrance? "I cannot distinguish its form, cannot invite it, as the one possible interpreter, to translate to me the evidence of its contemporary, its inseparable paramour, the taste" (I, 35). The "taste," which is also *smell* ("the smell and taste of things remain poised a long time"), necessarily accompanies the "form," which is the only "interpretation" or "translation." What is a visible form that serves to translate if not writing? If we recall that the remembrance scene is superimposable upon the masturbation scene and that the masturbatory act, in its turn, is at one level symbolic of the writing act, then it is obvious that the madeleine scene is ultimately, to borrow Derrida's expression, the *scene of Proustian writing;* and it is undoubtedly in the deepest sense that it is actually the matrix of the entire work.

Proust assigns the "remanence" or "odor" that Barthes attributes to speech to a material inscription in the object: "And so it is with our own past. . . . The past is hidden somewhere outside the realm, beyond the reach of intellect, in some material object (in the sensation which that material object will give us) which we do not suspect" (I, 34). The well-known formula, at first glance enigmatic or naive, according to which "the duty and the task of a writer are those of translator" (II, 109), takes on a new light in this context. It is a question not of passing from "life" to "book"—from the ineffable to language—but of translating a "subjective book of . . . strange signs" (II, 1001) into an exterior book of known signs: that is, to pass definitely from a spoken text (our existence) to a written text (our work). This movement from speech to writing, which is one of elucidation ("the true life . . . is literature"; Pléiade III, 895), seems in fact to be the one that is sketched (in an as yet unelucidated way) by the madeleine scene. Contrary to appearances, the chronological order (the past experience is prior to the work) cannot be confused with the functional order; if writing is the *language of translation*, it precedes another language in a virtual way, as the presence of the past in the object precedes the sensation that this object gives us.

The Barthesian metaphor is, then, the Proustian metaphor, displaced from writing to speech, deactivated because dislodged from literature, where Proust had installed it in the place of honor. If the madeleine scene tells us about the movement toward writing, the first *visible* manifestation of writing (in the form of a carefully elaborated metaphorical system) that follows it is olfactory: the baking of odors into an immense "puff-pastry" in Aunt Léonie's room (I, 38). Of itself, writing becomes allegorical here, so to speak.

But what is an "odor" of language? Proust answers us at the end of the "madeleine": "But when from a long distant past nothing subsists, after the people are dead, after the things are broken and scattered, still, alone, more fragile, but with more vitality, more unsubstantial, more persistent, more faithful, the smell and taste of things remain poised a long time . . . and bear unfalteringly, in the tiny and almost impalpable drop of their essence, the vast structure of recollection" (I, 36). This persistence of the personal past (memory of beings and of things) in a quasi-immaterial inscription (odor/"almost impalpable" writing) corresponds precisely to what Barthes describes as the "remanence" of speech: that is, its inevitable reference to "those illusions of experience, of memory, of feeling which occur to the subject that I am when I speak, that I was when I spoke." In this respect, the whole project of the *Recherche* can be contained within a transformation of Barthes's remarkably Proustian/anti-Proustian formula: "The subject which I am when I write (the Narrator) converts the experiences, the memories, the feelings which occurred to the subject that I was when I spoke (the Hero) from the illusory to the Real." In any case, we find ourselves back at the same question: what *trace* of a subject is there in language—odor symbolizing at best here the both evanescent and persistent quality of a presence/absence which is, as Proust says, "almost impalpable"?

We perceive, in the end—and this is undoubtedly why it has occupied us so long—that the Proustian madeleine is the matrix out of which issues not only the *Recherche* but also, even if it is by contrast, the contemporary problematic of writing. The "madeleine" is, in sum, the simple, foolish question that every piece of writing poses to every writer: *how is that (by, from) me?* When I write, I trace lines: where is *my* trace in them? In these sentences in which I have not invented a single word, where is *my* mark? Where *am I* then in my language?

It does not help to answer that the very idea of "trace" or "mark" is itself a myth, or that I am never "in" my words but "between" them; never in a discourse in which I speak but in that in which I am spoken. Whatever the way in which I situate myself in language, whatever the infinite mediations through which I can be grasped or the differential series in which only a certain deviation makes me manifest, I am certainly *there* somewhere. But in what place? And what might be the status of my presence? Again, it does not help to say that the very notion of presence is "metaphysical" and colored by "logocentrism." Besides the fact that a pejorative imputation has no value in argument, it really matters little whether the notion is true or false. Revealing an "illusion" is insufficient; the important thing is that it be, in fact, *possible*.

Proust believed that the work of art expressed the most "singular" identity of the artist, just as we have believed for centuries that writing, in the same capacity as painting, is an "imitation" of the real. The problem of the inherence of the subject and of the object of discourse within discourse is posed in analogous terms. Of

tion: Zola's fictions are not the "fictions" of Borges. Caught within an indissolubly denotative-connotative system of expression, the writer can manage (it is his "art") to underline one aspect and repress the other, to *pretend* to play one card and conceal the second, to privilege the "that was" or the "that was not" arbitrarily. It is even possible for the writer to play these two cards successively, the neurotic possibility of retroactive annulment being inscribed *within the nature of language* (to say in order to deny). This is the case with Proust who, after having achieved his work, manages to have it become a work to be achieved. All fictions, then, are far from identical. Some are naive and some are subtle (like lies), well constructed or poorly linked, coherent or incoherent, idiosyncratic or mythic. There are fictions that are conscious of their status (modern) or oblivious of their nature (classical). In short, a fiction can be more or less clever, just, moving, rich; it is never more or less "real." That is in fact why it is simply beating a dead horse to reveal *urbi et orbi* literature's illusion of realism or to display a pure aesthetic prejudice, since in any case literature's only reality is illusion. Aunt Léonie, more artful, has already enclosed us within an infinite meditation on the formula: the truth of a fiction is a fictional truth.

The object, then, is never present in discourse but is presentifiable in it through an imaginary act; what is false at the level of the real and of scientific analysis becomes true in the form of fantasy, where the gestures of writing and reading are located. The tree is indeed phantasmally *present* in the word "tree": it is of this word that literary forests are made. Despite the epistemological gaps that science opens among the three orders of signifier, signified, and referent, we can say that in the practice of language the ghost of the referent constantly haunts the domain of the signified. Even better, the signifier itself, the "tree," as analogon of an image-making act, functions as a "trace" of tree in discourse. The reason for the "counterdiscourse" which, according to Foucault, literature constitutes in the evolution of knowledge, lies undoubtedly in the persistence in the writer of the childhood belief in the omnipotence of thought—"the age," says Proust, "in which one believes

course we know that the word "dog" does not bark, that the word "table" can neither produce nor reproduce the table—words are not things. We know that with words *all resemblance is an illusion*. What remains to be explained, however, is the *illusion of a resemblance* which itself is an actual fact. That we can speak of a "good" or "bad" description, of a "faithful" or "fanciful" portrait, attests—in language itself—to our belief in a norm that allows us to judge whether or not this language is adequate to the exterior world. To prescribe with Flaubert that we should place ourselves in front of an apple tree and that we should write until the sentence takes hold of this very apple tree is a piece of advice that is by definition impossible. For all that, it is not absurd; it can be followed and can serve, for example, as a sorting device to choose words. Similarly, from Robbe-Grillet to Ricardou, critics struggle and wear themselves out in repeating that "realism" in literature is a distortion, a banalization, and a misunderstanding of the true goals of writing; nevertheless, a literature with a "realistic" aim is perfectly conceivable, and the proof is that it exists—that it even dominates.

The simultaneous and contradictory possibility that language possesses to designate the world by obliterating it and to obliterate the world by designating it cannot be transcended. What Jakobson explains in technical terms—"The supremacy of the poetic function over the referential function does not obliterate reference (denotation), but renders it ambiguous" (*Essais*, 238)—the Majorcan storytellers that he cites say even better in their habitual exordium: "That was and was not." The naturalistic "slice of life" is just as *unreal* as a surrealist poem, because of the simple fact that reading is an imaginative gesture. Imagining the marquise "leaving at five o'clock" or the Martians landing on earth are equally fantastic acts. If Taine defined perception as a kind of "true hallucination," it is equally true that a "false hallucination" is as necessary to imagine Julien Sorel climbing the scaffold as to see the "Peau de Chagrin" shrink. Zola is as fictional as Borges. Borges is no less *true* than Zola.

Of course, there are differences, though not degrees, in fic-

that one gives a thing real existence by giving it a name" (I, 69). This is an age which, in a certain sense, neither writer nor reader ever goes beyond, and which they share with the child, the primitive, and the obsessional neurotic—Freud *dixit*. The inherence of the subject in its written discourse seems to be of the same order; its *objective absence* (I am no more on the page than the tree) is a *phantasmal presence* (I haunt the horizon of words as the tree the groves of the poem)—with, however, a radical difference: whereas the *object* of discourse is never *there* in discourse (its real presence is a fantasy) the *subject* of discourse is never any place other than in discourse (its phantasmal presence is real). According to Benveniste's formula, "Whoever says Ego is Ego," there is no need to wonder how the "self" can "be translated" or "expressed" in words, since it is *in them*—at one of its levels at least—that the "self" is constituted. To the question "Where am I in language?" the answer is, "*I* is nowhere but through my language." *My* trace, *my* mark is not a particular sign within a verbal system, a distinctive or distinguished tic; it is the totality of my language (including, of course, the gestural) that can be distinguished from the language of others (as my body can be distinguished from other bodies). Some linguistic "unities" can be apprehended *en bloc:* La Bruyère of Proust and, although they want to be as "impersonal" as possible, Robbe-Grillet and Ricardou. All (nonscientific) discourse has a spontaneously "egological" structure to the extent that the ego is constituted in discourse and that there is no discourse without ego.

But how are we to understand this "egology" or, better, this "egophany" of language? This is actually the essential problem that Proust poses for himself and for us. The "writing-sperm" described in the *Contre Sainte-Beuve* as "a trail on the leaf, silvery and natural" (CSB, 31) is a trace belonging to *whom?* On this question he offers a theory in the well-known formula: "A book is a product of a different *self* from the self we manifest in our habits, in our social life, in our vices" (CSB, 100). It is this hiatus of self to self, this schism between the self and the other self, that is staged in the madeleine scene in the allegorical form of temporal difference. Now the remembrance scene tells us: this *other* is also *the same one.* I am not myself's other, as I am the other's other. This dialectic of the *trace* and of the *subject*, of the subject's trace, of the subject's place in the trace ("I feel something start within me, something that leaves its resting-place"; 1, 35), the *out-of-place place* of the subject—this is ultimately what the Proustian madeleine invites us to contemplate, and it can be resolved by nothing less than an entire philosophy.

More modestly, it is difficult to leave this text, all of which is *in the form of a question*—"Whence could it have come to me, this all-powerful joy? Whence did it come? What did it signify? How could I seize upon and define it?"—without attempting to sketch an answer. As a kind of receiver for a human being—for being—in language, psychoanalysis seems to be the most appropriate "resonance chamber" to amplify, to reverberate the underlying interrogation within the text. The question the writer poses to writing (where am I myself in that?) is that which the patient poses to his or her speech, through the analyst-receiver. What then does the latter say to us? If my language is "mine," if "I" am locatable in my language, it is surely not according to the ancient scheme in which speech would be the "expression" of an *already constituted* self in another order of reality, either physical or psychical. On the contrary, speech is an essential *moment* in the construction of a proper subject; after the assumption of self in the mirror image and the dialectic of identification with the Other, "language restores to it in the universal, its function as subject" (*Ecrits*, 2). If we follow Lacan here, *formed* in this way, the *ideal I* "situates the agency of the ego, before its social determination, in a fictional direction, which will always remain irreducible for the individual alone, or rather, which will only rejoin the coming-into-being [*le devenir*] of the subject asymptotically, whatever the success of the dialectical syntheses by which he must resolve as *I* his discordance with his own reality" (*Ecrits*, 2).

Reality is self-discordant to the extent that it is unreality, pursuing itself (tending to realize itself) through (symbolic) real-unreal activity. Obsession is not a particular form of "sickness" that affects a subject; it is *the* sickness of the subject, its being as the impossibility of being. Literature is caught within the obsessional structure, not because it manifests a flawed element in an individual psyche but because literature's formal flaw is its very own form, the form taken by subjectivity, by the history of a subject, and therefore always mythic, tending to unite contraries, trying to reconcile the irreconcilable. Totalizing meaning, remembering what is dismembered, making continuous what is discontinuous, synthesizing what is fragmentary—the desire of literature dooms it to the impossible. For art (for the subject of art), only the impossible is the real—and the real is impossible. The place for the true is only "in a line of fiction." An object that is specular, identity-related, symbolic, the subject acquires itself only ideally and asymptotically; the *self* grasps itself, structures itself only as fantasy.

It is probably the analyst's illusion that the subject can be dislodged from illusion. Even though analysis provides indispensable points of reference, it cannot offer a refuge; the "strong self" of American neo-Freudians and also undoubtedly the Lacanian Other of the Pact, guarantor of Speech, the entrance into the symbolic order as a resolution of imaginary fascination—these are theoretical ramparts that analysis constructs to contain its own anxieties. The Freudian desire to substitute the "reality principle" (the order of Anankè, of Logos, a beneficial ascesis of Restraint and of Science) for the "pleasure principle" of the (foundational) primary processes does not constitute a concrete or even conceivable goal for analysis. Such a goal can no more be realized than the Lévi-Straussian desire to use a metonymic language that leaves no residue in order to "soak up" metaphorical language. The obsessional form of the analytic process itself will show, if need be, that it does not depart ultimately from the subjective, intersubjective, interphantasmal structure, to the study and understanding of which it has so effectively contributed.

Writing as an essential, not accidental, dimension of language is a mode, among others, in which that "line of fiction" of our subjective being is constructed. And certainly the "stages" (assumption of your own image, identification with the Other, entrance into the order of language) in no way form a harmonious continuum of a dialectical synthesis. The *self* is lodged in the hiatus of these irreducible registers; it resides in models of being that are not superimposable; it constitutes this difference from self to self that Proust so keenly felt, a detachment in time of an identity equally scattered among its strata (banal self, self of writing). The flash of remembering, the joy of remembrance that abolishes the feeling of being "mediocre, contingent, mortal" does not for an instant come to me from a fusion between internal and internal. My past—me, if time is me myself—"is hidden somewhere outside the realm, beyond the reach of intellect, in some material object (in the sensation which that material object will give us) which we do not suspect" (1, 34). My past is dispersed throughout the world, the object of chance meetings. The Narrator, in the madeleine experience, *meets* the past in the precise sense that the writer *finds* words.

In concluding, we must make more precise what we have already felt. This scene, at its last (or first) level, is a *mise-en-scène* of writing. If the only "material object" in which the writer is really hidden and potentially presented to himself is words, then the story of the erotic madeleine tells us about the long, delicious, and uncertain coupling of the writer and language:

I compel my mind to make one further effort, to follow and recapture once again the fleeting sensation and that nothing may interrupt it in its course I shut out every obstacle, every extraneous idea, I stop my ears and inhibit all attention to the sounds which come from the next room. And then, feeling that my mind is growing fatigued without having any success to report, I compel it for a change to enjoy that distraction which I have just denied it, to think of other things, to rest and refresh itself from the supreme attempt. And then for the second time I clear an empty space in front of it. [1, 35]

The rigorous pursuit of detail relates with clinical precision the very process of writing. The signifier clearly appears just before the consummation of the act: "And each time the natural laziness which deters us from every difficult enterprise, every *work* of importance, has urged me to leave the thing alone, to drink my tea" (1, 35). Here the "enterprise" is the "work."

"And suddenly, the memory appeared to me." This "visual" memory, linked to a "taste"—which suddenly "rises up" beyond "the echo of the great spaces traversed"—is *the form and the taste of words*. The writer does not find them when he looks, but once he is given these words, he recognizes them immediately. Writing is for him remembering. The interior is the anterior; his whole language is somewhere, already there, "hidden, out of his domain and his reach." And it is true that writing is a "gift"; words are always given to us. It is not at all our memory that creates our writing by "calling forth" words; our memory, on the contrary, is verbal matter. Our past is "in the sensation which that material object will give us"; there is sensation, taste, and form in *words*. As a speaking object, I have a memory and associations that are entirely linguistic. My *self* appears (reappears) when the signs become paired: a metaphorical movement occurs between two terms; I possess the "being-in-between," the Proustian *trompe-l'oeil*, which is undoubtedly less illusion than allusion. If "whoever says Ego is Ego," I am *displaced* in language; just as "I" am present in the place where my physical motility leads me, "I" am in the place where words transport me. The writer is the one who constitutes a *self* by substituting a body made up of letters for a physical body (something Proust well understood when he concealed the Narrator's person). More precisely, the writer tries to give himself/herself his/her own body in a body of work. You never have your own words as your own, of course; they always and already belong to others. In the process of writing, you are expropriated in advance (this is allegorized at the end of the *Recherche* in the theory of the "reader of yourself"). Yet if I am laced through and through by alterity in the corpus of my language, I am no less alienated in my physical body; I am no less dispersed in billions of cells than I am disseminated in the infinity of signs. No less, certainly, but *no more*. If I can say "my body," if I am *me* through my body, then I can say *my work;* I can be *me* through my work. *"Me" is that, right there.* Nowhere else, and nothing else. It is a process of totalization in which a totality is impossible; a synthesis constantly pursued and never to be found; a scattering indefinitely gathered together and then undone; life in which death is immediately at work. "*I*" is a permanent war against *the Other*: of food, of sex, of language.

With remarkable intuition Proust assigned to his "madeleine" the role of symbolic support for identity; eating, digesting, "making"—such is the rhythm of the conversion of the Other into the self, but also of the loss of the self in the Other. The "greatest" work has the status of this "little thing" that Freud talks about. It is altogether and by definition *attached* and *detachable*; it is mother-child, shit-me; it is my phallus. The "drop" that bears "unfaltering . . . the vast structure of recollection" is my sperm-ink, the tip of my pen-penis. Fantasy, certainly—but fantasy is *my* reality. The mythic narrative of the work's "creation" in the madeleine is the true narrative of the matrix of every self. Fiction of fiction, that is truth: "After the people are dead, after things are broken and scattered, still alone, more fragile, but with more vitality, more unsubstantial, more persistent, more faithful, the smell and taste of things remain poised a long time" (1, 36). Words have smell and taste—metaphorically speaking, of course. But their being is metaphorical, and so is mine. Meta-phorical, transporters of meaning; also, remanence of the object and of the subject at the two extremes of their chain. My words bear my odor and my taste, my words smell *of me*, to the extent that I have smelled *myself* in them.

Again, this is not expressionism according to which a being is constituted somewhere other than in language and then transferred into words—a kind of linguistic "mimesis." My language does not express me; it constitutes me. It is not a copy or a decal of me; it *is* me—one of *my* selves. I have spares (for changing myself)—which cannot be exchanged one for the other; which oppose each other without ever becoming superimposed; which mutually mimic each other without ever being able to unite, to unite with me. Because I am not. I exist, without being. I exist in the place where I am not. Such is my imaginary status. I exist, then, in this language, where I do not express a shade of being. I fully adhere to this fragmented, disseminated absence of myself. These pages which are printed, manufactured—this book which is paginated, fabricated at the pole opposite my body, beyond what is visible or legible to me, is of ME. The dispersion of the text, the depthless sparkle of signs gather together in the flash of a signature. "I" IS Marcel Proust. Not because we can show some "resemblance" between the "Narrator's" life and that of "Marcel Proust" (in this scene, the Narrator is no more Marcel Proust than Julien Sorel is Stendhal) but because the scriptor who signs Marcel Proust —in the very gesture by which he *detaches* from his own body the filaments of writing that he underlines by giving as the source of his text a colorless, odorless "I"—*attaches* himself to the new, printed body that bears and supports him.

To write is to transport myself from one body to another, to have (the) meaning (that I am) literally transformed. Yet I am this meaning without ever being able to incarnate it; I pursue it without ever being able to unite with it. Nothing *identical* is transported from one register to another; my *identity*, in each form, becomes transformed. Illusion, allusion. Identity is no less able to be grasped or located, however, for being fictional. It is in vain that Mallarmé tells us: "Impersonified, the volume, as much as one separates oneself from it as author, does not demand the approach of the reader. As such, keep in mind, among human accessories it occurs alone: made, existing. The buried meaning stirs and has all of the leaves at its disposal, as a kind of choir."[51] The "buried" meaning is that of burial; it is given as a metaphor of itself, a translation—always unfinished, partial—of *Mallarmé-text* (in the sense in which Freud talks about the individual patient as a text to be read) into *Mallarmé's text*. A translation makes occult, it conceals. To impersonify the volume, Mallarmé effaces the historical and stylistic person, "the personal, enthusiastic direction of the sentence" (p. 366). Of course, this does not deny that the Mallarméan sentence is the most rigorously controlled, and not always in the way the poet understands: "The Penultimate is dead"; "the inexplicable Penultimate" is not so buried that she cannot be exhumed and, being the *next-to-the-last* dead, not so inexplicable that Mauron cannot read in her the dead mother who is at the (buried, repressed) center of the work.

Yet a reading that lifts the repression does not, for all that, lift the "death-work." If the poet is doomed to be in mourning for the Penultimate-mother, it is not because of a simple biographical accident; to write, you have to "say farewell" to an original life, a mother-life, a mother-source, a mother-tongue. It has become one of the banalities of our culture to say that as an author, you die to your language, that the act of writing demands your death. We must be more precise: if writing is to change bodies, then dying, for the writer, is to pass from one body to another.

The insistence of this same metempsychosis opens the *Recherche* with that "Other Scene" in which the connected destinies of dreaming and writing are acted out:

I had been thinking all the time, while I was asleep, of what I had just been reading, but my thoughts had run into a channel of their own, until I myself seemed actually to have become the subject of my book: a church, a quartet, the rivalry between François I and Charles V. This impression would persist for some moments after I was awake. . . . Then it would begin to seem unintelligible, as the thoughts of a former existence must be to a reincarnate spirit. [I, 3]

And certainly we will not be surprised that for the child of the Combray "readings"—if the spontaneous posture of the reader is that of the sleeper: "I would be lying stretched out on my bed, a book in my hand" (I, 63)—reading is one of the forms of dreaming, dreaming a prolongation of reading: "I had been thinking all the time, while I was asleep, of what I had just been reading." Dream of reading, dream/reading. What does the reader dream of? Of being a writer. Nowhere can Proustian circularity be more easily grasped than where it does not know that it is present. The first words of the text constitute the last word of the *Recherche* (which Proust dreamed of calling *La Vie revée*, "The Dreamed Life"): "I myself seemed actually to have become the subject of my book."

From the word go, the *Recherche* will act itself out through a play of signifiers. It is written in a musical score, in a certain *key*—a key of dreams, hidden from the novel itself: "*It would begin to seem unintelligible*"—a key that analysis attempts to provide.

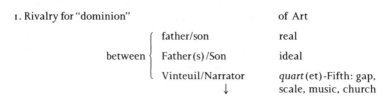

CHURCH	→	metaphor of the Book → place of music	
QUARTET	→	sonata sep*tet*	→ Vinteuil

RIVALRY BETWEEN FRANCIS I AND CHARLES V

1. Rivalry for "dominion" of Art

between
- father/son — real
- Father(s)/Son — ideal
- Vinteuil/Narrator ↓ — *quart*(et)-Fifth: gap, scale, music, church

2. Rivalry between *signifiers*

(a) music/language

{ sonata
"played" septets
music

{ sonata
"written" septets
book

"I asked myself if Music were not the unique example of what might have been if there had not come the invention of language, the formation of words, the analysis of ideas—the means of communication between one spirit and another" (II, 560).

(b) writing/speech

Francis I
↓
"writer" will work
like *François(e)*
(II, 1114)

/"speakers"
↓
Charles V
Charles (Swann)
Charl(us)

3. Rivalry between *subjects*

French (*Françoise:* embodiment of France I, 116)	foreigner barbarian, Jewish

War between

France	Germany, Austria (*Temps retrouvé*)

Great War between

self	the Other

The material certainly is "the thoughts of a former existence": "All these materials for literary work were nothing else than my past life" (II, 1016). To go from the past state to the oneiric state (continuity of the intelligible), you nevertheless have to pass through a radical break (discontinuity of being), "as after metempsychosis." In the writing of dreams and of works, the protean ability *to-be-other* demands the abandonment of *being-yourself*: "*I myself seemed actually to have become the subject of my book: a church, a quartet.*" A book is literally that: church, quartet—a *sonorous architecture.* "*I myself seemed actually to have become the subject of my book*": my book is *me* on the condition that I *make* myself *other.* To make myself other, *to be myself*: in search of myself, from existence to existence, from dreaming to working, from a body of flesh to a body of print. Psychoanalysis can do many things, but not this one—abolish metempsychosis. Interpreting my dream is possible only if I am not the dreamer. Dreaming is possible only if I can no longer be the interpreter. "*Rivalry between François I and Charles V*": I am split, divided once again among instances of myself which are fighting.

We know that these famous wars finished with a tie. To dream, to write, I abandon myself; I make myself other. But the other about whom I write, I dream, is me. A vicious circle, and it spins. You cannot get out. You shouldn't get out. The literary object, Sartre *dixit*, is this top: to stay up, it has to turn in a circle from one contrary to the other, from a fantasy to its opposite. *I, it, cannot be Marcel Proust. Marcel Proust is necessarily I.* "Watch the ferret run": this is the game played by the Narrator and the young girls at Balbec. You think you have caught it. It catches you, does not stay in one spot, moves from one to the other, comes back to the same person. I am caught. The Other replaces me. "Stunned with grief, I let go the cord, the ferret saw that ring and swooped down on it, and I had to go back into the middle, where I stood helpless, in despair, looking at the unbridled rout which continued to circle round me" (I, 690). Ferret. The squirrel-script, by spinning in the obsessional cage, makes the cage spin. To spin or turn here is to return: the Petites Madeleines, the Proust Marcel, to Marcel Proust.

Proustian precedence of the maternal first name over the law of the father and the order of the state. Language mixes the names without shaking the structure. Petites Madeleines, P(roust) M(arcel): conscious project (be yourself); unconscious desire (be the Other). R(obbe-Grillet, icardou): conscious project (not be a self); unconscious desire, trace of the signature (not be an Other). The terms can be turned around by history, without being overturned. We know that a dream is an unfulfilled wish; we also know that the subject is represented in every dream. Now if I always dream of, about, myself, it is precisely because I never manage to be myself. Thus I offer myself to myself in the writing of dreams as in the dreams of writing, in the same mode or model, which Proust has shown to be nutritive. Insatiable feeding. The conclusion is what we find at the beginning. Matrix of the book: what originally and immediately makes the MADELEINE emerge is, naturally, the word

FAIM.

Afterword

Doubrovsky's *Place de la Madeleine* has been a controversial text in the history of Proust criticism, and there is every reason to believe that its scandalous qualities will have new life now that the text is easily available in English translation. Many of Doubrovsky's first-time American readers might resent his rudely insistent analysis of Proust's famous madeleine scene, with its ruthless exposure of Proust's fantasies as the phantasmagoric parade of all "writing."

Doubrovsky could give double scandal to American readers of modernist fiction raised in the decorous traditions of Trilling, Levin, Booth, and Shattuck: his *Place de la Madeleine* both violates the practices of academic critical discourse and traces throughout the novel the tendrils of Proust's anal-erotic fantasies from that initiatory spot at the beginning of the text to their place in the intertextual fantasies of all fictions of the self. Doubrovsky adapts Lacan's rewriting of Freud's Oedipal theory to do a psychocritical analysis of the *text*—that is to say, *not* of the biographical Proust who pens the novel but rather of the textual creature, the "posited author," whose existence is a function of the differences between the narrator and the biographical "Proust" toward whom the text seems to be gesturing.[1] Much could be said of Doubrovsky's contribution to Proust criticism in correcting the humanistic reading of the novel which—in its desire for established subjectivity—identifies the narrator with the "biographical author." Most important, though, is the way Doubrovsky's psychocritical reading highlights the conflicting conscious and unconscious textual functions of the novel to show how comically out of Proust's control the *Recherche* can be seen to be.

Indeed, the strengths and weaknesses of Doubrovsky's text center on the question of the subject. On the one hand, he demystifies critical notions about the nature of "authority" by showing the "author" to be, in part, a textual function; but on the other hand, he tends to neglect the historicity of the *Recherche* and of the subject's dissipation with which he is concerned. Although Doubrovsky's text is roughly contemporaneous with Foucault's and Derrida's investigations into the nature of "authority" in literary and philosophical writing, it is fundamentally unaffected either by the critique of metaphysics or by the investigation into the conditions for discursive practice.[2] While Doubrovsky has considered Derrida's thinking about the question of the subject, especially about the difficult status of the "proper name," he is deeply indebted to the Lacanian psychoanalytic tradition and resists the implications of Derrida's powerful demonstration that Lacan's retention of truth as the articulation of desire reinscribes his psychoanalysis within the domain of metaphysics. In fact, rather than accepting Derrida's critique and moving away from Lacan, Doubrovsky embraces the Lacanian position that Derrida attacks—precisely to show in his reading of the novel that the "subject," the "posited author," cannot but speak the "truth," that is, speak symptomatically. Indeed, the Lacanian techniques serve Doubrovsky well in letting him read Proust's novel as the symptomatic field of play for the inescapable fantasy of writing's recovery of origins and authority. Of course, the symptomatic reading necessarily uncovers all the various impossibilities of such a project, but it does so only to show, again and again, that it is the articulation of a desire—in the unavoidably distorted forms literature subtends—that is simultaneously "truth" and "lie." It is this insistence upon exploring desire and its Oedipal manifestations and systemic appearances which can lead Doubrovsky to formulate the various paradoxes about the truth of the lie throughout his reading.

But it is not Doubrovsky's avoidance of the radical Derridean critique that should most interest us.[3] Rather, given the political concerns of the 1980s, we should perhaps emphasize the critical narrowness that follows upon Doubrovsky's dehistoricizing of Proust and the authorial problematic. In other words, we should triangulate the recent history of criticism to position Doubrovsky in relation not to Lacan and Derrida primarily, but to Sartre and Foucault. Of course, this is not the only possible positioning. One could, for example, quite usefully take Doubrovsky's work as a rewriting of Deleuze's study: the latter's reading of Proust's novel as a "critique of Philosophy" could then be seen to have been displaced into Doubrovsky's more scandalous "critique of Literary Criticism"—Doubrovsky insists again and again that all interpreters are unavoidably caught up in the same psychodrama which he finds unearthed for us in Proust.[4] He reverses the fundamental claim of Deleuze's study: for Doubrovsky there can be no unexamined critical desire for completed aesthetic form to substitute for the stability of style. Since for Deleuze, style cannot be a function of a unified subject, it must find its own unity elsewhere—and not from "essence." "What then," asks Deleuze,

is this very special mode of unity irreducible to any "unification," which appears afterwards, which assures the exchange of viewpoints as it does the communication of essences, and which appears according to the law of essence, itself alongside others, a final brushstroke or a localized part? The answer is as follows: in a world reduced to a multiplicity of chaos, it is only the formal structure of the work of art, insofar as it does not refer to anything else, which can serve as unity.[5]

Deleuze strongly desires to establish the integrity of Proust's text as part of his larger plan to show the complex intertextual unity of all writing. This desire requires Deleuze to invent the new concept of "transversality" to ground the possibility of the formal closure of the *Recherche*. He posits it as the necessary condition not only for the integrity of Proust's text but also for the interrelationships between otherwise closed and integral texts which, as he sees it, structure the intertextual unity of all writing.

Doubrovsky essentially replaces this semiotic category with an equally systematic psychoanalytic one which more effectively grounds itself in the experience of the body and the fundamental forms of social life: namely, the family and sex. Yet despite the relatively greater value of a concept that recognizes the priority of the body and sexual-familial life in the understanding of literary fantasy, Doubrovsky's use of the notion is somewhat disappointing: his conceptions of sex and family are surprisingly ethereal and transhistorical in this work. Just how free-floating his concepts are becomes obvious—as I shall try to suggest—when the *Place de la Madeleine* is read alongside Sartre's *Idiot of the Family* and Foucault's various archeologies and genealogies.

But despite the limitations of Doubrovsky's concepts, his rewriting of Deleuze is critically and politically useful: it calls our attention once more to some of the problems in the kind of position held by the Frankfurt School, especially by Adorno, regarding the aesthetic realm's priority in a world of degraded and indeterminate sign systems. That is to say, Doubrovsky's text poses a major challenge to various culturally conservative adaptations of Freud's theory of sublimation. He demonstrates how little productive of desirable cultural and moral order even the apparently most successful sublimations actually are. Doubrovsky precisely shows, in opposition to Deleuze—and we might add Adorno and Trilling—that the so-called aesthetic unity of Proust's novel is itself a fiction generated by a narrative, indeed, by writing itself as part of its own hypocritical attempt at self-justification and self-authorization.[6] Furthermore, by studying the process of "translation" by which Proust's text reformulates the Oedipal structure in a narcissistic masturbatory fantasy, Doubrovsky has shown how aesthetic writing is in a sense, a contaminant: it spreads its desires and hallucinations through a population to whose own fantasies it appeals ideologically. In other words, to adapt Althusser's adaptation of

Lacan, these translated aestheticized fantasies "colonize" the unconscious of the critics and critical discourses that rise up to feed upon them, to attempt to appease their own desires. But the effect of these feedings, of these ingestions, is, in Doubrovsky's terms, either great effort for little reward or endless and anomic spewing of desire in unstable and deceitful critical echoings. In revising Deleuze, then, Doubrovsky can be seen to revise the entire Anglo-American tradition of critical interpretation and cultural value production. Taking Doubrovsky seriously would be scandalous indeed!

While Doubrovsky's psychocritical reading of Proust advances beyond the metaphysics of Deleuze's reconstitution of an all-too-familiar formalism, it does so at the cost of denying the critic of Proust the opportunity to historicize the novel or the critic's own analysis. Doubrovsky's decision to move in the direction of Lacan, despite his evident interest in Sartre's existentialism,[7] comes increasingly to appear in Doubrovsky's work as an attempt to revise the late Sartre, especially the *Critique of Dialectical Reason* and *The Idiot of the Family*, with their emphasis upon the possibility of a materialist biography and dialectical cultural history. In other words, Doubrovsky's *Place de la Madeleine* represents one major aspect of structuralist and poststructuralist renunciations of Sartre and, with him, of the French left's commitment to dialectical historical models of interpretation and practice. In effect, Doubrovsky's decision not to treat historically the problem of the subject or the narcissism of *écriture* and instead to treat the text as a relatively timeless space, as an almost Heideggerian "field" of play or, perhaps better, as a structuralist grid of systemic functionings—all these choices mark the post-'68 turn from Marx and his tradition toward linguistically synchronic models that fundamentally privatize the complexities of cultural production.

It is rather disappointing that Doubrovsky does not follow as far as he might along Lacan's vector in analyzing the social nature of the Symbolic. He does not adequately consider the interaction of the Imaginary and the Symbolic in the social order; instead, he treats these categories as if their boundaries were the psyche in itself and as if language were not a social category. At the origin of Doubrovsky's decision lies the assumption that the psyche and *écriture* are transcendent terms isolatable for psycho-grammatological study. As I shall try to suggest, one problem with this approach is that it blocks critical discussion of the social inscription of the novel in the *historical* dimension of language and writing.

Of course, Doubrovsky's psycho-grammatological emphasis has the apparent advantage of breaking with and out of the kind of interminable analysis to which Sartre's project would commit criticism. Doubrovsky can offer a relatively complete account of the coming into being of Proust as writer without the need—but also without the opportunity—for what Sartre discovered theoretically and practically to be the impossible project of inscribing a writer as complex as Flaubert (or as "pure" as Flaubert) within a dialectical representation of his historical totality.

But what should we think of this advantage? Has the *Place de la Madeleine* not found its "adequacy" precisely at the expense of Sartre's sublime vision of what the critic cannot accomplish? Or to put the matter more professionally, we might ask whether Doubrovsky can enable the multiplicity of texts, the sheer amount of critical discourse, that Sartre might if he were taken as a critical guide to what yet needs to be done. There is, if you will, a finality to Doubrovsky's accomplishment which is its weakness as well as its strength. What Sartre struggled and failed to find—the "unique origin" of a writer's call—Doubrovsky, without recourse to any phenomenology, has been able to represent by severing Proust's text from its historical inscription; by this act of radical ascesis, he has freed the critic/reader into the possibility of producing (endlessly) new readings that recount the circulation of a text's signs around and through the system of its guiding fantasies.

There is a simple and traditional way to consider this issue: can we say that Doubrovsky's revision of Sartre makes possible "readings" that add to knowledge? This ancient question, long authorized by the discourses of humanism and the ideology of capitalism, has of course been under serious attack from poststructuralism and feminism, especially from feminists for whom "theory" is an essentially male exercise of power. Nonetheless, the question can be posed in somewhat different terms that restore its legitimacy. We might ask if it makes any difference whether critics produce essays which are, like Doubrovsky's, self-admitted narcissistic fantasies (for that is all critics can produce within the circularity of psychocriticism) or whether they research, like Sartre, the various conditions and contexts for the production of any or all cultural artifacts. Of course, we know that critics like Hayden White[8] find it possible to describe every call for contextualist scholarship as a "trope" of irony to accompany what he would see as certain necessary and predictable liberal, cultural, and political values; yet the claim to such a possibility is not in itself demonstrative and so does not in any way preclude the opportunity or lessen the need to make a critical judgment about the political and professional consequences of producing one kind of text or another. If, for example, Perry Anderson is correct in any sense, in his Wellek lectures about the reactionary character of the French move against Marxism since the 1960s,[9] then Doubrovsky's decision to try to subvert Sartre's great and necessarily unfinished project must be approached with caution by American intellectuals who, in the age of Reagan, hope to continue the revision of the American institution of literary and cultural studies and to understand its place within North America's imperialist culture.

While Doubrovsky's very powerful reading of Proust's novel captures and displaces the interminable nature of Sartre's project into the professional aura of the "effective performance,"[10] it can do this only by noting its own inscription within the system of Oedipal fantasies it finds embroiling all writing, and by failing to mark its own entanglements within the much more culturally complex sets of institutions and discourses that support and enable its own existence and distribution. Here the name of "Foucault" must serve as a sign of Doubrovsky's and certain poststructuralists' turning away from the task of doing a history of their own possibility and position.

What Sartre has attempted for Flaubert, Foucault in a sense attempts for the genealogy of the human sciences. Of course, there are critical differences between dialectics and genealogy that cannot be elided (or worked out here.)[11] But there is an overriding similarity that differentiates them from Doubrovsky's project: in different ways both were committed to the historical research necessary to produce knowledge about and some control over how we have come to be where we are, especially as intellectuals involved with structures of power and oppression present in state domination and cultural hegemony.

Now that Doubrovsky's *Place de la Madeleine* is available to English-speaking North American literary critics, it should be easier for the academy to understand how complex have been the results of the French turn from Marx. The broader political implications of the movement have been the subject of repeated analysis. But perhaps the most salient feature of this turn—at least for North American critics—has been its textual and theoretical productivity. Only somewhat less apparent is the *ascetic* nature of this turn. As I have been trying to suggest, Doubrovsky's *Place de la Madeleine* is worth serious attention because it nicely represents the productive nature of this ascesis and gives us a clear sense of its nature. We might say that it is an allegory of criticism's unavoidable inscription within certain inescapable and endlessly enabling (because obsessive and "textual") fantasies. But that allegory, we must recognize, depends—in Doubrovsky's own terms—upon a certain ascetic conception of criticism which limits its range of subject and action to an infinite repetition of the same.

The essential point here is twofold: the North American professoriat is always searching for new models and rhetorics, new "issues" and "problems" to fuel its productivity; Doubrovsky provides *both* a model that lends itself to reproduction *and* an argument that legitimates the critical expectation that nothing but such (professional) narcissicism is possible within the fantasy-controlled world of writing revealed by psychocriticism. Most important, Doubrovsky's *Place de la Madeleine* encourages its audience to forget its own historical specificity, and so its asceticism will be welcome within the profession and will lead, ironically and necessarily, to its own reduction to a further (narcissistic) legitimation of the status quo, of the regulative protocols of North

American literary criticism and pedagogy. Once the *Place de la Madeleine* is positioned in this way, we may see how it might be taken up in the United States: to reenforce a profession that too often rewards simply the ability to perform well and often.[12]

The professional consumption of Doubrovsky would forget how the crises of 1968 and the established left's failure to develop answers to pressing political and theoretical problems[13] called forth such texts as Doubrovsky's and how they should be studied for clues to what can be done now to restore some of the critical intelligence and political understanding lost in the defeats of the sixties and the seventies—and that there has been such a loss is what the seemingly endless need for critical ascesis most readily reveals. Above all, though, the professional appropriation of texts like Doubrovsky's must not be allowed to go unchallenged, or they will simply come to reenforce the ruling critical ideology of advanced academic literary intellectuals under Reaganism: that is, they will function as yet another license for critics to settle into the "unavoidable" space of transforming fantasies within which "criticism" "duplicates" the textual problems it "reveals" (and within which it too is "always already" inscribed).[14] Of course, as I have already suggested, such an ideological function would support a (seemingly paradoxical) productive quietism: critical "readings" everywhere, but politically radical critical knowledge nowhere. Such a "license" hardly positions North American (particularly white male) intellectuals to challenge the rising conservative hegemony or to understand their own place within it.

Perhaps the importance of Doubrovsky's text inheres less in its contribution to the history of Proust studies per se than in the general political history of post-'68 critical intellectuals, and particularly in that chapter which will tell of North American adaptations of French structuralist and post-structuralist projects to a different nation's political program at a time of crisis in its imperium. The repeated American "depoliticization" of various French critical projects can be somewhat misleading, for it allows us to forget the political and ideological role such "depoliticizations" play within the discipline and so within the culture. We can say one thing with certainty: they support the continuation of an essentially conservative profession, and support as well the structuring system of reward and punishment the profession sets up for its practitioners. Doubrovsky's *Place de la Madeleine* has its greatest value when read in light of the struggle to see how this structure functions, and how the discipline and critical intellectuals are positioned in North America. In other words, its importance is not as documentary evidence of the brilliance with which Lacanian psychocriticism can engage with what it takes to be the failed ghosts of Marx and his heirs; but rather as a quite wonderful instance of how critical intelligence, when faced with what seems to be a decrease in its available resources, will struggle to find new ways to deal with the past and its own impoverished situation in order to carry out its most serious critical projects. In North America, though, we must always be cautious lest the profession to which we belong forget the lesson of Doubrovsky's inventiveness and conveniently discover in his work merely another legitimation for its nonreflexive, nonpolitical practices and protocols.

Notes

TRANSLATOR'S PREFACE

1. Serge Doubrovsky, *Corneille et la dialectique du héros* (Paris: Gallimard, 1963); *Pourquoi la nouvelle critique? Critique et objectivité* (Paris: Mercure de France, 1966), published in English as *The New Criticism in France*, trans. Derek Coltman (Chicago: University of Chicago Press, 1973); *La Place de la Madeleine: Ecriture et fantasme chez Proust* (Paris: Mercure de France, 1974).

2. *Le Jour S: Suivi de "Chronique américaine," roman discontinu* (Paris: Mercure de France, 1963); *La Dispersion* (Paris: Mercure de France, 1969).

3. See my "Proust and Psychoanalytic Criticism," Ph.D. diss., State University of New York, Binghamton, 1979, ch. 1.

4. See William V. Spanos, "Modern Literary Criticism and the Spatialization of Time: An Existential Critique," *Journal of Aesthetics and Art Criticism* 29 (1970): 87–104.

5. See Bové, "Proust and Psychoanalytic Criticism," ch. 2; and Pierre V. Zima, *L'Ambivalence romanesque: Proust, Kafka, Musil* (Paris: Sycomore, 1980).

6. René Girard, *Mensonge romantique et vérité romanesque* (Paris: Grasset, 1961).

7. Jeffrey Mehlman, *A Structural Study of Autobiography: Proust, Leiris, Sartre, Lévi-Strauss* (Ithaca, N.Y.: Cornell University Press, 1974).

8. Gilles Deleuze, *Proust et les signes* (Paris: Presses universitaires de France, 1970).

9. See Milton Miller's *Nostalgia: A Psychoanalytic Study of Proust* (Boston: Houghton Mifflin, 1956). For a very brief analysis of the *Recherche* as a novel changing in time, see Leo Bersani, *A Future for Astyanax: Character and Desire in Literature* (Boston: Little, Brown, 1976).

10. See also Paul de Man, "Criticism and Crisis," in *Blindness and Insight: Essays in the Rhetoric of Contemporary Criticism* (New York: Oxford University Press, 1971), 3–19.

WRITING AND FANTASY IN PROUST

1. Volume and page references are to C. K. Scott Moncrieff and Frederick A. Blossom's translation, *Remembrance of Things Past*, 2 vols. (New York: Random House, 1932–34). Short, undocumented quotations (aside from a few that I have translated myself and those I have retained in French) are also from this edition. Except for a few words in French, the italics—unless otherwise noted—are Doubrovsky's. The footnotes that follow are my own.

2. Marcel Muller, *Les Voix narratives dans "A la recherche du temps perdu"* (Genève: Droz, 1965). All page numbers are from this edition; the translation is mine. Unless otherwise indicated, translations of the many other writers cited by Doubrovsky are mine also.

3. Philippe Lejeune, "Ecriture et sexualité," *Europe* 502–3 (1971): 113–43. This article is hereafter cited in the text by page number.

4. All quotations from *Contre Sainte-Beuve* are from Sylvia Townsend Warner's translation in *Marcel Proust on Art and Literature: 1896–1919* (New York: Meridian Books, 1958), hereafter cited as CSB.

5. The capitals and *coquille de Saint-Jacques* appear in the three-

volume Pléiade edition of the *Recherche* (Paris: Gallimard, 1954), I, 45. Later notes concerning the French refer to this edition.

6. The French exactly repeats the words *si mince* (so thin): I, 668; III, 11.

7. The French (I, 47) begins "*après la destruction des choses*" (after the destruction of things).

8. The French uses the very terms "enter"/"exit," *entrer/sortir*, in the "marquise's" invitation, "Vous ne voulez pas entrer?" (I, 492), and in the reference to Combray, "Tout Combray . . . est sorti" (I, 48).

9. The French version of this quoted expression was a Revolutionary catchword; see Warner's translation: CSB, 400.

10. Gérard Genette, "Proust et le language indirect," in *Figures II* (Paris: Seuil, 1969), 223–94.

11. There is an additional allusion to the sacred in the original: "gossamer" in the CSB passage quoted above appears in the French as "fil de la Vierge," literally, "Virgin's thread."

12. Jacques Lacan, *Ecrits: A Selection*, trans. Alan Sheridan (New York: Norton, 1977), 199; hereafter cited as *Ecrits*.

13. The French is *spectacle* in both the episodes described above.

14. Page numbers refer to Marcel Proust, *Pastiches et mélanges* (Paris: Gallimard, 1947).

15. Marcel Proust, *Jean Santeuil*, trans. Gerard Hopkins (New York: Simon & Schuster, 1956), 586.

16. Gaëtan Picon, *Lecture de Proust* (Paris: Mercure de France, 1963), 61.

17. Gérard Genette, *Figures I* (Paris: Seuil, 1966), 47. All references are to this edition.

18. Samuel Beckett, *Molloy* in *Three Novels* (New York: Grove Press, 1965), 7, 64–65, 134. Subsequent page numbers from this edition are given in the text.

19. Samuel Beckett, *Proust* (New York: Grove Press, 1931), 47. Page numbers in the text refer to this edition.

20. Sigmund Freud, *The Interpretation of Dreams* (New York: Avon Books, 1965), 435. Subsequent references are to this edition.

21. Roland Barthes, *Nouveaux Essais critiques* (Paris: Seuil, 1972), 127–28; hereafter cited as NEC.

22. Claude Lévi-Strauss, *The Savage Mind* (Chicago: University of Chicago Press, 1969), 214. Subsequent page numbers refer to this edition.

23. Serge Gaubert, "Proust et le jeu de l'alphabet," *Europe* 502–3 (1971): 68–83.

24. Sigmund Freud, *Totem and Taboo*, trans. A. A. Brill (New York: Random House, 1946), 75. Subsequent page numbers refer to this edition.

25. Doubrovsky's remarks here apply only to the French version (I, 45), where "Petites Madeleines" is capitalized.

26. Gilles Deleuze, *Proust and Signs*, trans. Richard Howard (New York: Braziller), 120. Page references are to this edition.

27. Jean Rousset, *Forme et signification* (Paris: Corti, 1962), 157.

28. Roman Jakobson, *Essais de linguistique générale* (Paris: Minuit, 1963), 180; hereafter cited as *Essais*.

29. Emile Benveniste, *Problems in General Linguistics*, trans. Mary E. Meek (Coral Gables, Fla.: University of Miami Press, 1971), 172; cited hereafter as PGL.

30. Oswald Ducrot and Tsvetan Todorov, *Dictionnaire encyclopédique des sciences de langage* (Paris: Seuil, 1972), 321.

31. Claude Lévi-Strauss, *Structural Anthropology*, trans. C. Jacobson and B. G. Schoepf (New York: Basic Books, 1963), 216.

32. Guy Rosolato, *Essais sur le symbolique* (Paris: Gallimard, 1969), 48–49.

33. Sigmund Freud, *Cinq Psychanalyses*, trans. Marie Bonaparte and Rudolph Loewenstein (Paris: Presses universitaires de France, 1966), 301; hereafter cited as CP.

34. Jacques Derrida, *Of Grammatology*, trans. Gayatri C. Spivak (Baltimore, Md.: Johns Hopkins University Press, 1976), 108.

35. Maurice Blanchot, *La Part du feu* (Paris: Gallimard, 1949), 315; hereafter cited as PF.

36. Sarah Kofman, *L'Enfance de l'art: Une Interprétation de l'esthétique freudienne* (Paris: Payot, 1970), 117. All references are to this edition.

37. Claude Lévi-Strauss, *The Raw and the Cooked* (New York: Harper & Row, 1970), 5. Page numbers refer to this edition.

38. Sigmund Freud, *The Complete Introductory Lectures on Psychoanalysis*, trans. and ed. James Strachey (New York: Norton, 1966), 295.

39. *Essais de psychanalyse*, trans. S. Jankelevich (Paris: Payot, 1963), 192.

40. Jean Laplanche and J. B. Pontalis, *Vocabulaire de la psychanalyse* (Paris: Presses universitaires de France, 1967), 484.

41. Charles Mauron, *Introduction à la psychanalyse de Mallarmé* (Neûchatel: Baconnière, 1968), 173.

42. Jean-Paul Sartre, *Situations*, vol. 9 (Paris: Gallimard, 1972), 45; hereafter cited as s.

43. Michel Foucault, *The Order of Things* (New York: Random House, 1973), 43–44.

44. Sigmund Freud, "The Relation of the Poet to Day-Dreaming," in *On Creativity and the Unconscious*, ed., Benjamin Nelson (New York: Harper & Row, 1958), 46.

45. Maurice Merleau-Ponty, *The Essential Writings of Merleau-Ponty*, ed. Alden Fisher (New York: Harcourt, Brace & World, 1969), 227.

46. Jean de La Bruyère, *Les Caractères* (1688; rpt., Paris: Garnier, 1962).

47. *Sexuality and the Psychology of Love*, ed. Philip Rieff (New York: Collier Books, 1974), 91.

48. From a 1908 letter to Madame Emile Straus, reprinted in the appendix to Doubrovsky, *La Place de la Madeleine*, 187.

49. Sigmund Freud, *The Problem of Anxiety*, trans. Henry A. Bunker (New York: Norton, 1963), 15.

50. Roland Barthes, "Ecrivains, intellectuels, professeurs," *Tel Quel* 4 (1971): 11; subsequent pages are cited in the text.

51. Stephane Mallarmé, "Variations sur un sujet," in *Oeuvres Complètes*, ed. Henri Mondor and G. Jean-Aubry (Paris: Gallimard, 1970), 372; subsequent pages are cited in the text.

1. For a study of the "posited author," see Michel Foucault, "What Is an Author?" in *Language, Counter-Memory, Practice*, ed. Donald F. Bouchard, trans. Sherry Simon and Donald F. Bouchard (Ithaca, N.Y.: Cornell University Press, 1977), esp. 129; originally published in *Bulletin de la société française de philosophie* 63, no. 3 (1969): 73–104.

2. Ibid., 113–38. See also Jacques Derrida, *Of Grammatology*, trans. Gayatri Chakravorty Spivak (Baltimore, Md.: Johns Hopkins University Press, 1976), 107–18; originally published as *De la grammatologie* (Paris: Minuit, 1967).

3. As I hope to make clear, in this context Doubrovsky has more in common with Derrida than might at first appear: the work of the latter has already been, and that of the former might well be, adapted by a North American professoriat anxious to legitimate its "nonpolitical" protocols.

4. Gilles Deleuze, *Proust and Signs*, trans. Richard Howard (New York: Georges Braziller, 1972).

5. Ibid., 149.

6. We should add, of course, that both Adorno and Trilling were extremely conscious of the instability and fragility of beauty in the modern world; see, e.g., Lionel Trilling, "On the Teaching of Modern Literature," in *Beyond Culture* (New York: Viking Press, 1965), 3–27.

7. Serge Doubrovsky, "The Nine of Hearts: Fragment of a Psychoreading of 'La Nausée,'" trans. Carol Mastrangelo Bové, in *Psychoanalysis, Creativity, and Literature: A French American Inquiry*, ed. Alan Roland (New York: Columbia University Press, 1978), 312–23.

8. Hayden White, *Metahistory: The Historical Imagination in Nineteenth-Century Europe* (Baltimore, Md.: Johns Hopkins University Press, 1973).

9. Perry Anderson, *In the Tracks of Historical Materialism* (London: Verso Editions, 1983). I hope it is clear that I am not sub-

scribing to all of Anderson's objections or recommendations about the future of the left.

10. See Jean-François Lyotard's critique of "performativity" in *The Postmodern Condition*, trans. G. Bennington and B. Massumi (Minneapolis: University of Minnesota Press, 1984), 54ff.; originally published as *La Condition postmoderne* (Paris: Minuit, 1979).

11. See Paul A. Bové, *Intellectuals in Power: A Genealogy of Critical Humanism* (New York: Columbia University Press, 1986), esp. ch. 1, "Mendacious Innocents, or the Modern Genealogist as Conscientious Intellectual."

12. See David Lodge's wonderful parody of criticism's obsession with multiple orgasms in *Small Worlds* (New York: Macmillan, 1985), 324–25.

13. See Anderson, *Historical Materialism*, 27–31.

14. For a discussion of some of the points of intersection of Reaganism with criticism's textual obsessions, see Edward W. Said, "Opponents, Audiences, Constituencies, and Community," *Critical Inquiry* 9 (Sept. 1982): esp. 22ff.